D1554412

INFINITE WAY LETTERS

The
INFINITE WAY LETTERS 1955

By
Joel S. Goldsmith

DeVorss & Company, Publisher

Original British edition published in 1955
DeVorss & Company reprint, 1992

ISBN: 0-87516-641-5

DeVorss & Company, Publisher
P.O. Box 550
Marina del Rey, CA 90294

Printed in the United States of America

"Except the Lord build the house, they labor in
    vain that build it."

(Ps. 127.)

"Illumination dissolves all material ties and binds
men together with the golden chains of spiritual
understanding; it acknowledges only the leadership
of the Christ; it has no ritual or rule but the divine,
impersonal universal Love; no other worship than
the inner flame that is ever lit at the shrine of Spirit.
This union is the free state of spiritual brotherhood.
The only restraint is the discipline of Soul, therefore
we know liberty without license; we are a united
universe without physical limits; a divine service to
God without ceremony or creed. The illumined walk
without fear—by Grace."

CONTENTS

INTRODUCTION

MANY attempts have been made to teach the Infinite Way through a mail course, or series of lessons, but none have succeeded.

In our particular work success has come through the personal relationship which naturally exists between Teacher and student, *if* the student has been spiritually led to the Teacher, and also if the Teacher does not humanly seek students. My great joy is the relationship I enjoy with students and it has naturally followed that those with whom I could not be personally present, must be inspired by means of correspondence.

Study well my original book *The Letters*, and *Infinite Way Letters* of 1954 and 1955, together with the Writings, and you will quickly see how the bond thus established between student and Teacher results in definite inspiration and inner unfoldment. It must become clear to all students that the greatest inspiration and spiritual progress will come to those who are spiritually guided to their Teacher and teaching. Pray, pray, pray—for spiritual Light and direction until YOUR Teacher is revealed to you. Then follow diligently, sacredly and secretly in the inspiration that unfolds to you, and one day your spiritual progress will be shouted from the housetops.

For those on the Infinite Way, the Monthly

Letter is the point of contact between Teacher and student, and through them every bit of fresh inspiration which comes in our daily work is shared with students instantly, all over the globe.

At present these Letters go into over three thousand homes in the United States and Canada, and about seven hundred in England. Some travel to the continent of Europe, of Asia, Africa and Australia; thus students are united in study and meditation and naturally benefit by "two or more" being in one Consciousness—of one Spiritual Household.

Do you see now that these Letters constitute a bond between you and me, and between you and every student seriously studying and living The Infinite Way? Do you realize that you can travel through many lands, near and far, and find a welcome from those accompanying us on the Infinite Way of Life? "We are no more strangers"— we are one in the fellowship of the Spirit.

You will be greatly helped in your spiritual life if you will spend a few minutes each day in meditation to realize the Presence of God, and then to "feel" that this One-ness with God constitutes your one-ness with all spiritual being. This Divine Union brings the entire spiritual universe into your individual experience.

Aloha greetings,

JOEL.

P.O. Box 5041, Pawaa Station,
Honolulu 14,
Hawaii, U.S.A.

CHAPTER ONE

THE IMPORTANCE OF MEDITATION

OUR work is to live in God; to dwell in the secret place of the most high; to keep thought stayed on Him; to pray without ceasing. Throughout all ages, the scriptures of the world have given us this same truth: "If ye abide in me, and my words abide in you, ye shall ask what ye will, and it shall be done unto you."

No part of the Message of the Infinite Way is more important than meditation, for it is only through meditation that we are enabled to find God. There is no other way. The act of meditation is solely for the purpose of quieting us into a state of peace and serenity, in which we become receptive to the Word of God unfolding and revealing Itself in and as our consciousness.

Each of us has many moments during the day and night in which to abide in the Word of God, to meditate upon Truth, be it only a momentary pause during our work, before meals, while walking, driving or resting. If wakeful during the night, we can spend that time with God and find rest in His peace. While we are dwelling in God no sense of evil can come nigh our dwelling place.

God is the all-knowing Mind, so take the attitude that He knows our needs better than we do, and turn within only for the impartation of His Word.

We may be meditating because of a lack of health, or supply, or companionship, but it is not necessary to enlighten God. Just turn to Him with the expectancy of an impartation from within, and the Word of God will be made flesh—it will appear outwardly in human experience, and therefore let us not be concerned as to what form it shall take.

There may be times when no thoughts come, but be grateful: thoughts are not necessary. "My peace I give unto you. . . ." Be satisfied with the sense of peace that is beyond words and thoughts and knowledge, and relax in it. Thank you, Father, I rest in Thy peace. Thy Grace is my sufficiency. I am happy, peaceful, joyous in Thy peace. The kingdom of God —the Allness of God is within me.

In this meditation we do not think of ourselves, we do not ask God for anything, we have no hopes, no wishes, no ambitions. We rest in the Spirit, in God's Presence, His promises and assurances, and in this consciousness awaken to the realization we have been desiring. "Therefore be ye also ready: for in such an hour as ye think not the Son of man cometh."

"Man shall not live by bread alone"—not by the truths we think or declare or read, "but by every word that proceedeth out of the mouth of God," and the only way to hear that Word is to listen. Seek, ask, knock, but do not acquaint God with the nature of the problem. Leave your problems outside the door, and enter into the sacred place to hear the still, small Voice, with the attitude that you are seeking only the kingdom of God.

Should any difficulty arise, become still and quiet

inside. At such times as it may appear that you have some need or human requirement on the outer plane, no matter what the claim, let your answer be: "I have meat to eat that ye know not of." Refute all temptation to yield to the claim of lack with the Word of God, which is your meat, your wine, your water, your home eternal in the heavens.

In this understanding you can be reborn. You can undergo a change of consciousness wherein are needs you long to have fulfilled, to a consciousness that faces every claim with "I have meat to eat that ye know not of." In this consciousness you are aware of the Word of God—the invisible substance of all form, the essence of which every demonstration is made. In this consciousness you have the bread of life, the wine of inspiration, the invisible source of supply, the fount of all good; and as you turn within and feel Its Presence, It manifests outwardly as demonstration.

While this new consciousness is forming, you may, for a while, be faced with some sense of limitation or delay which may cause you to doubt the Presence of the Christ, and it is then you need to remember: "I will never leave thee nor forsake thee. . . ." It is in quietness and *in confidence* that you rest in assurance. If you have even a grain of faith, the Christ will see you through. Your good can appear outwardly only in proportion to the development of spiritual consciousness within. Disaster results from accepting appearances and feeling that perhaps you do not deserve God's blessings, and that He is not paying attention to your needs. If you will learn to sing in prison and never to fear, even in the valley

of the shadow of death, you are acknowledging that
"I *have* meat"—the Word of God—and that will
bring you through all forms of discord.

Many times we may feel that error is responsible
for our inharmonies, and in so doing we violate the
first commandment. All power is in God. The darkness of discord may be a step to bring us to God,
for God works in mysterious ways to give us the
lessons and, thereby, the blessings we need.

Father, Pray

"Likewise the Spirit also helpeth our infirmities:
for we know not what we should pray for as we
ought: but the Spirit itself maketh intercession
for us with groanings which cannot be uttered."

(Rom. 8:26.)

This may seem a startling statement, but *you do
not know how to pray*, and if you are obedient to the
Voice of the Spirit you never will know how to pray!
The further along the Spiritual Path you travel, the
nearer you come to the place where you let God do
the praying, and it is then you let the Spirit pray in
you, bear witness, make intercession for you. God
knows far more about prayer and what to pray for,
what you need and how to present it than you do.
You know not what to pray for; you know not how
to go out or how to come in; you know not what
your need will be tomorrow. Therefore, the only way
you have of praying is: "Father, pray. Reveal Thyself, the activity of Thy Being in me and through
me. Let the Spirit make intercession for me."

In one of my recent writings, I made much of the

fact that the "I" is a devil. The personal "I" which calls itself Joel, or Mary, or Bill, is really a devil, because it takes unto itself powers it does not possess. The word "I", wrongly used, can interfere with your demonstration, and even the thought that "I can give a treatment", or "I can pray", can be a hindrance. Much better results follow when you have learned to make your statements of Truth merely for the sake of raising yourself in consciousness. When you come to that period of quiet, of listening, of peace, say: "Father, I know not how to pray, nor what to pray for. I know not how to pray to become free of disease or discord." *Then let the Father pray!* Let the Father reveal the activity of *His* thoughts. "For my thoughts are not your thoughts, neither are your ways my ways, saith the Lord." Therefore, listen to the Lord's thoughts, and let the Lord have His way in you.

You come to a very high state of spiritual illumination as you realize that you do not know how to pray, and that all you can do is to learn to listen and let the Father reveal Himself within you. All power is in God, so let us be receptive and responsive to that Power and Presence of God, and It will do all things through us—even pray! It will not answer *our* prayers; It will not fulfill *our* desires; *but It will fulfill Its own desires in us!*

My Peace

"Peace I leave with you, my peace I give unto you: not as the world giveth, give I unto you. Let not your heart be troubled, neither let it be afraid."
(John 14:27.)

I would like you to meditate upon this statement for many days to come—a week, or two or three—until the Father within reveals to you what the Master meant when He said, *"My* peace" . . . not as the world giveth. . . ." The world has the power to give you only a human sense of peace. You might call it an absence of war and animality, an absence of hate and revenge. But that is not *"My* peace." *"My* peace" is a very spiritual thing. It is something that can better be understood through the word "Grace." It is a state of peace that has in it no thought of humanhood or human values—it is a state of divine being.

You can bring this state of divine being into your experience. You can, through pondering and meditating upon this statement, ultimately achieve an awareness of its inner meaning, and find within yourself this state of Grace descending. In scripture, this state of Grace is called the descent of the Holy Ghost. It is a release from humanhood—from human standards and values, and even from human good. It is something higher than human good—it is something divine; it is something not of this world; it is something straight from God.

Prayer

Prayer, in The Infinite Way acceptance of the word, is totally unlike the accepted dictionary meaning of petitioning, supplicating, beseeching.

While pondering words and all their varieties of meanings, my thought turned to how these words came into being: how feeling had first become caged in the form of words, and so became generally accepted to have much the same meaning the world over. In thinking of the feelings embodied in certain words, I was then in a state of meditative prayer.

In this quiet, contemplative state my thought turned to the Psalms of David, and how his Psalms were prayers. Many times he poured forth his personal sense of anguish, remorse, doubt, but always he came back to the understanding of his true relationship to God. Then his prayer became a song of praise and thanksgiving, and awareness of his relationship to God.

Prayer then can be a cleansing agent, a clearance of old beliefs, a "cleansing of the temple," and sometimes this cleansing can take the form of a whip—a lash to drive out the belief that our bodies can be other than "the temple of the living God."

Only the Christ performs this type of prayer, because only the Christ knows when the temple is being desecrated. The natural man can give many good reasons why the money-changers should be in the temple. So, then, an important function of prayer is listening for the Christ—silently, expectantly listening for Its interpretation, and then following through by obedience.

Only those of pioneer dispositions or with an adventurous spirit within can get the utmost from prayer. The word itself, having a supplicatory association, would disguise this fact, but anyone having explored the path of prayer for any period of time can tell you it is a glorious new adventure in living—the opening up of an heretofore unexplored realm. The dropping away of horizons is perhaps the first step; then old concepts slough off, one by one, and you begin to find you have never known your "Self."

Try it, and through the gateway of prayer, "Acquaint now thyself with Him, and be at peace: thereby good shall come unto thee."

(A Student.)

The Power of Secrecy

"Take heed that ye do not your alms before men, to be seen of them: otherwise ye have no reward of your Father which is in heaven. Therefore when thou doest thine alms, do not sound a trumpet before thee, as the hypocrites do in the synagogues and in the streets, that they may have the glory of men. Verily I say unto you, They have their reward. But when thou doest alms, let not thy left hand know what thy right hand doeth: That thine alms may be in secret: and thy Father which seeth in secret himself shall reward thee openly. And when thou prayest, thou shalt not be as the hypocrites are: for they love to pray standing in the synagogues and in the corners of the streets, that they may be seen of men. Verily I say unto you, They have their reward. But thou, when thou prayest, enter into thy closet, and when thou hast shut thy door, pray to thy Father which is in secret; and thy Father which seeth in secret shall reward thee openly."

(Matt. 6:1-6.)

Secrecy is one of the profound and powerful principles of harmonious and joyous living, and only those who have discovered the world of secrecy can realize its beauty, peace and Grace.

Rightly understood, The Infinite Way reveals that we do not pray, but rather that God utters His Word—and it is done. We do not pray: we *hear* the "still, small Voice" declaring His Truth within us, *and this is prayer*. Only in Silence, and "in the secret place of the most High" can we become aware of the Divine Presence, and thereby be in prayer. And this prayer is openly fulfilled in the harmonies, joys and peace of our daily experience.

". . . do not sound a trumpet before thee, as the hypocrites do in the synagogues and in the streets, *that they may have the glory of men . . . they have their reward*." Indeed, to give alms, to give assistance and to share, brings a reward in the regard of men. But to do these secretly is to gain the Grace of God, the recognition of Love, and thereby God's bounty is openly received. The reward for praying in public is in the regard received from men, but only those who have learned to pray "in secret" may experience the Grace of God *in answering prayer*.

To give, or to pray, where others may witness and possibly praise, is to glorify self, and this is a violation of Christ's Law. The law of self is eliminated when the gift and the prayer are secret. God is the only Giver, and so praise of the self, or glory drawn to the self, leaves one outside the realm or benefit of the Law. Giving in secret is the recognition of God as the real Giver, and thereby the glory rightly belongs and goes to the Father.

When fasting from the indulgences of the senses, we are not to make evident to the world that we are refraining from the world's standards: instead, let us appear outwardly as men, while living inwardly as Saints. Hereby Spiritual Law is fulfilled.

It is possible to observe this principle or its violation in our own experience. For a few days take heed, and mark how much of self is praised, thanked and recognized in the acts of giving and praying. Then for a while, give and pray in secret where no one can know the source of the benefits received, and notice now how self, self-benefit and self-glory have been absent and, naturally, how all recognition and praise is given to the Divine Source of all Good. It is in this deflation of self that the Christ is fulfilled.

The Master teaches much of praying for our enemies; for those who despitefully use us and persecute us; for those who do evil. This manner of prayer is but the recognition of God as the Father, the Life and the Law unto *all* men; the awareness that God's Love to His Children is evidenced in much forgiveness; the realization that Christ holds no man in bondage to his sins, but graciously utters, "Neither do I condemn thee . . . Thy sins are forgiven."

How but in secret and in silence can we receive such wisdom from the Father, and feel such love for mankind—even those who hate us? If we voice such sentiments aloud, is it not merely that we may be praised for *our* great spirit of love and forgiveness, whereas actually we are but the instruments through which *God's love and God's forgiveness* reaches the world?

Since "the earth is the Lord's and the fulness

thereof . . ." actually we have nothing to give to anyone, that is, nothing that belongs to us, except by His Grace. Is it not fitting then that our giving be in secret that only the Father may receive thanks, praise and glory? Thus the elimination of the self is the fulfilling of Love's Law.

We are admonished: "Thou shalt not bear false witness against thy neighbor." Spiritually, we understand this to mean that we are not to judge man by appearances, but consciously to know and understand the spiritual nature of his being; to recognize Spirit as the law and source and activity of individual being. To look upon man as he appears to be—mortal, material, finite, sick, well, rich, poor—is to bear false witness against him. To recognize and realize Christ as the true identity of everyone, and to understand Love as man's true nature, is to pray for him.

Each day it is our privilege and duty to retire into our secret chamber of consciousness, and pray this prayer of realization for those of our household, our business, our community, our nation, and this *giving* of our understanding, of our time and our devotion will be rewarded in His Grace literally appearing as our sufficiency in all things.

Daily Inspiration

In order that we may fill ourselves with the Spirit of God, which is the wine of inspiration, the living water that is to spring into newness of life, we must empty ourselves of whatever thoughts, beliefs and opinions that act to separate us from the Presence and the Power of God. Before this inspiration can flow, and before we can receive the assurance of

God's Presence and Power, we must empty ourselves of our conceits, our egotisms, and our beliefs that we, of ourselves, are sufficient to live this life. To bring this about—this emptying of ourselves—we turn to scripture: "Trust in the Lord with all thine heart; and lean not unto thine own understanding. In all thy ways acknowledge him, and he shall direct thy paths."

Never has prayer gone unanswered. Never has anyone prayed and not received an answer and a blessing. We may doubt this because we earnestly believed that we have prayed. Many times we believed that we have lived constantly in prayer, but now we learn that we have prayed amiss unless we have gone to God with an understanding of the nature of God and the nature of prayer.

When we declare that we are to lean not unto our own understanding, but that we are to acknowledge *God* in all our ways, we must know how this is to be done. And so we turn to the Master, and seek from Him guidance in the understanding of the nature of God and prayer. In the 12th Chapter of Luke, we read: "And he said unto his disciples, Therefore I say unto you, Take no thought for your life, what ye shall eat; neither for the body, what ye shall put on. The life is more than meat, and the body more than raiment. . . . For all these things do the nations of the world seek after: and your Father knoweth that ye have need of these things. But rather seek ye the kingdom of God; and all these things shall be added unto you. Fear not, little flock: for it is your Father's good pleasure to give you the kingdom."

Here we see that we are not to ask God for the things of the world, because He *knoweth* we have need of these things. Perhaps it is in this way that we have failed in our understanding of prayer, because if we have asked God for safety, security, peace, supply or employment we have prayed amiss. God is the all-understanding Mind, the all-wise Father, the Divine Intelligence of the universe, and it is absurd to tell Him of our needs.

We also see that God is Divine Love, because it is His good pleasure to *give* us the kingdom. It is not God's will that we want or lack for any good, nor is it God's will that we petition and beseech for our good. Just as it is our great pleasure to give to our children, much more so is it the pleasure of the Father to give *us* all that is necessary for our good.

Now that we know something of the nature of God and something of the nature of prayer, we can relax. Be still, be silent, and from the depths of this inner Silence comes the Spirit which appears as our cloud by day and our pillar of fire by night. From the depths of this inner Silence comes forth the healing water that brings everlasting life. From the depths of this Silence comes the Peace of God, and once this peace has descended there is nothing to fear: the prayer is complete—"Fear not, little flock."

All prayer or communion with God is for only one purpose—to achieve this sense of peace within; to achieve the realization that ". . . lo, I am with you alway." Let us have that sense of Divine Presence *now* and we will have answered prayer. Let us fail to achieve this sense of peace and the prayer is not a prayer. The feeling of the Presence is in itself a prayer.

Let us understand this: our problem is at an end, not when we think *we* have found a solution, but when we have *felt this inner peace.* In "My Presence" the fires do not burn, the waters do not drown, the storms do not rage. The power of Christ is the answer to every form of discord.

Above all, let us remember that *God* is the all-knowing Mind, the ever-loving Father who knows our every need, even before we do, and that it is His good pleasure to *give* us the kingdom. And as we ponder the revelation of the Master, we will hear it said within our own being: "I will never leave you nor forsake you." "My Presence" goes before you. Lean not unto your own understanding —*acknowledge this Presence!*

GRACE

THERE is an area of consciousness through which you are instantly one with God, and with all spiritual being and creation, and through which you find instantly available all forms of good. This has been described as a Sea of Spirit, and it is as well the universal or divine Soul. In achieving conscious contact with this Sea of Spirit (or the Father within) you find divine Love pouring Itself into expression, so that you no longer live by personal effort alone, but by Grace. Rather than to seek your good from persons or things, tap this universal Soul and become a beholder as It pours forth as ideas, manifest as the human forms of good so necessary to your present experience. It is only as you learn to look to this Infinite Invisible that you begin to understand the nature of Grace.

Instead of seeking or desiring something already existing as form or effect, learn to turn within and let your good unfold from this divine Source, the Infinite Unseen. Let the practitioner and teacher seek activity from this inner source. Let the business and professional man look to the divine within. Let the sick and the sinner seek healing and perfection from within. Be ever alert, expectant of Consciousness unfolding as new and richer and lovelier forms of good, and you will experience the abundance of life—by Grace. To understand that your

Soul is the eternal storehouse of all good is permitting the activity of the Christ to function in your experience through Grace.

What is "the Father"? The Father is universal Consciousness; the Substance of all form; divine Mind acting as your mind and manifesting as limitless ideas; immortal Life appearing as the harmonies of individual life. Seek everything in life from the kingdom within. Draw your good from the infinity of your own being. Touch that center, the kingdom within, and let the Father reveal your heritage. *This is to live by Grace.*

Grace is the gift of God. The Children of God live by Grace: we are heirs—"heirs of God, and joint-heirs with Christ." The Father reveals, "Son, thou art ever with me, and all that I have is thine." Grace may be summed up as a release from all human desires in the actual understanding and achievement of spiritual realities.

Most men and women have a measure of faith that there is a God, a divine Power. However, to some there comes a conviction (or actual *realization* of God) which is termed an experience of Christ, after which their lives are lived by Grace. This spiritual experience is also known as illumination, or rebirth. In mystical literature it is sometimes spoken of as Cosmic Consciousness or Christ Consciousness. Those who have attained this Light have no further "problems" of existence, since they are fed, clothed and housed from the infinite inner Fountain of Life we call Christ.

The secret of Grace is contact with the Infinite Invisible, the universal center of being within you.

The earnest seeking of the realization of the kingdom of God, through reading and studying inspirational literature and scripture, and through frequent pondering and meditating on God and God's creation (leading to actual communion with the Father within) brings to your consciousness the touch of the Christ. "Thou wilt keep him in perfect peace, whose mind is stayed on thee; because he trusteth in thee." This leads to an awareness (sometimes, even a Voice) and some day you will know that ". . . he performeth the thing that is appointed for me," and then Grace will have taken over in your life. This moment of Grace cannot be adequately described, since it appears in different ways to different people, but all who have received this Light understand the experience of the illumined of all the ages.

While the bibles of all peoples contain numerous true stories of the miraculous experiences of the illumined, the activity of the Christ, resulting in living by Grace, is by no means limited to the past. More than ever before, untold numbers of men and women have experienced the Christ, and are now living lives of beauty, health, harmony and joy— by Grace. With Truth now available to all who can read, spiritual illumination is a possibility to every earnest seeker. To live "not by might, nor by power, but by my spirit," it is only necessary to earnestly desire a knowledge of God. "Acquaint now thyself with him, and be at peace." The moment you receive the realization of the Father within, the moment you "feel" the atmosphere of Love, which is an inner awareness of the Presence, that is the beginning of your life by Grace.

True Humility

The advent of the Christ in the consciousness of
Jesus of Nazareth was accompanied by the deep
humility that forever after made Him deny personal powers, personal virtues and personal honors
in His conviction that "I can of mine own self do
nothing . . . the Father that dwelleth in me, He
doeth the works. . . . My doctrine is not mine, but
His that sent me. . . . If I bear witness of myself,
my witness is not true." These statements of the
Master reveal a deep inner conviction and awareness of something invisible (the Father within)
accomplishing the mighty works of healing, redemp-
tion, and feeding the multitudes on the outer plane.
"My Father worketh hitherto, and I work . . . I
and my Father are one . . . my Father is greater
than I." Wherever you find one who has been
touched by the Hand of the Divine, you will find
this same realization of an Infinite Unseen . . . yet
all power is expressed in the realm of the visible.

As you come to this place in consciousness, you
feel that your life has been taken over and is being
lived *for* you, as well as *through* you and *as* you.
It is as though the Presence were always going
before you to "make the crooked places straight,"
and the desert "blossom as the rose," and to open
doors of opportunity, of service, and of welcome.
It is not that you, of yourself, have these powers,
but rather that "the Father that dwelleth in me,
He doeth the works." As you observe more and
more of the activity of the Christ in your consciousness (ever appearing as more beautiful and wonderful thoughts, manifesting as greater and still greater

deeds of spiritual power) your trust and faith grows by leaps and bounds.

From the moment you receive this inner conviction, you relax and rest—*and let the invisible do the works*. No longer do you *use* Truth to overcome error, but *let* Truth appear as the activity of your consciousness. As you come to the realization of God as the only power, you learn that neither sin, fear nor disease have any power, and you give up the struggle against every form of discord. To relax the human power, the personal will, the mental or physical might, is to obtain "by my spirit".

Paul achieved a life by Grace as shown by the deep humility expressed in his words, ". . . I live: yet not I, but Christ liveth in me . . . I can do all things through Christ which strengtheneth me." To live by Grace enables you to do greater things, and to achieve better results in all your activities, because of this spiritual impulsion and divine guidance. Concern for your personal welfare (or for that of your families or nations) cannot be dropped, except when this inner Wisdom reveals itself to you; freedom from fear, danger, or lack can only come as the Comforter appears. The Voice of Truth utters Itself within you, and It becomes the "Peace, be still," to every storm in your experience.

Christ Consciousness is "this mind . . . which was also in Christ Jesus," voicing Itself. You must cultivate It. A few people are born into the world with some measure of Christhood, but everyone may develop and cultivate this awareness to the degree of his fidelity to study and meditation. Your receptivity consists in keeping open the passageway of

31

consciousness, so that you may recognize and welcome the Christ as It touches and awakens your Soul into newness of life. In the silence of your being Christ speaks, and you hear: "I will never leave thee, nor forsake thee . . . I am with you alway, even unto the end of the world." This consciousness of God's Presence is developed in quietness and stillness, in patience and perseverance; by abstaining from mental power or physical might, so that "my spirit" may function *as* your life. "Be still, and know that I am God."

"For by grace are ye saved through faith; and that not of yourselves: it is the gift of God. . . ." By Grace are *you* saved!

There are no Added Things

"I listened, and the Voice told me what to do"— meaning the Voice, still and small, or loud and insistent, that speaks sometimes in moments of meditation. We all know that when we have a problem, a situation in which we do not know how to act, the best and wisest thing is to go into meditation. We know, too, that we must leave the problem outside, as the Orientals leave their shoes outside the door, and very often the solution is there, with our shoes, as we come out. Seldom is the solution in the form of concrete instructions, although sometimes even in that form, but the sense of release, the removal of strain, worry or doubt is a frequently known thing. We know that God is not with humans, that God cannot give advice on matters of health, supply or happiness. Yet God does speak, and in speaking guides our human destiny. To what extent, actually, has the Voice spoken, to what degree of detail has the instruction amounted?

The answer, here, is one that is based purely on interpretation and, indeed, every answer must be based on that. "In what language did God speak to you?" is a question that has been asked of saints and seers. And the reply to that is that the saint understood God *without* language, and proceeded to translate or interpret that wordless understanding into his own language. And it is on the degree, the quality of the interpretation—both in the interpreter and in the receiver of the interpretation—that the degree of validity must rest.

No message from God is an Absolute one. It cannot be, because there is the translation or interpretation, and the need for communication, to stand in its way. There is the question of how it is to be described or put into words at all. The mystics have grasped, groped and tormented themselves on these lines: they have made denials, they have used parallels from the language of human love, and paradox phrases about dazzling darkness and formless forms. There is the problem of how to choose words that *you* will be able to understand.

The teacher himself, in his capacity of teacher, is an interference, a screen between God and the receiver. Even the idea of any persons involved at all, is an interference. God must speak His own message wordlessly, and to no one. It is picked up, translated, and then delivered from one man to another, and at once there is a concept—a false concept—taking place. This is true even of the Biblical texts that we like to think of as being permanent and absolute. They have been written down, translated from one tongue into many others; they have gathered meanings and interpretations acquired through the centuries. From a spoken word, which was an attempt to convey a wordless thought, they have been passed down into the phrases that we are always trying to see through and beyond.

To pursue this thought to its ultimate is finally to deny validity to all expression, and to retire into a soundless, trance-like state. In the meantime, what are we to do about the present state of affairs, where the translation is all there is, even though we may know that it is never an accurate one? The best we can do is to accept that fact, but, remembering it, to try and train ourselves, our minds and our spirits, to be better translators, to be recipients whose sense of the meaning behind the words is as fine and as high as we can make it. And, especially, never to reach for that interpretation, never to seek it as such, but to listen only for as wordless and intangible an understanding of God as can be made known to us, and never for the message or for the use that the message can bring to us.

This use, this sense of a worldly fulfillment, or a demonstration, not only may seem to happen, it almost always will happen in the earlier stages. The seeker after God, still living in the human world and obsessed by its problems, will find these problems lifted, eased and clarified. Then, as he grows wiser, he will find, with some dismay, that the record of demonstration seems to grow less, and he will begin to wonder what is wrong. We know, now, only too well. "Ye pray amiss."

As we learn more and more about prayer, we realize more and more how easy it is to pray amiss. There is not one of us now who does not know that one must never pray for things, for persons or for healing; that God cannot change any physical thing; and that matter, as a solid and real entity, will never change under the use of Spirit. That far we have progressed. But there is another danger. We know that we must seek first the kingdom of Heaven, but we also remember that "all these things shall be added unto you." It is hard to forget that promise. We know that we must not seek these things, that our mind and spirit must be seeking the kingdom of Heaven only—but there is always the thought that if we find God all these *things* will be added. As has been stated in The Infinite Way Writings of Joel Goldsmith: *"There are no added things in God. God is the Thing Itself."*

That is true. I quote Mr. Goldsmith again: "When we hear the Master's words: 'I am come that they might have life, and that they might have it more abundantly,' do we not immediately think of a greater sense of human health and wealth?" Yet since human health and wealth are the things we know best, it is not strange if they become the symbols of abundance. But let us, at least, recognize them as symbols, and never as the real thing. When a problem is solved, when the deliverance is showered upon us, let us be careful never to regard that occurrence as the demonstration. Let us not think that God arranged it for us.

This must be true of all the things that the Voice seems to tell us. We must listen, and obey what we think we have heard, but we must never forget that what we have heard is a human interpretation only, and that that is not what we are after. Especially, we must make no effort towards that translation. Too easily we can go wrong, swung and swayed by our human wills and desires. When we know what we have heard, we know it! When we try and guess, try and interpret, we are more than likely to guess wrong.

This is all akin to the razor's edge of dilemma that exists in these matters when we try and understand them from a human plane. On the one hand, there is the absolute willing and seeking after God, a turning to God for nothing but God, with a wish to lose one's sense of self in the realization of one's Self. That is the furthest we can aim for. But in the meantime (and at the same time) one is—or seems to be—a human being living in this world, and one cannot more than momentarily forget that. And when one returns from that forgetting, there will be human needs and crises once again, problems and troubles that stand in the way of peace and clearness of Spirit.

Once, one would have taken these problems to a practitioner, asking for their dispersal as such. Still, if one cannot achieve a clear vision that dispels them, one will ask for help, *for the removal of the troubled spirit, the disturbed or limited consciousness that cannot find peace, that cannot find God.* And when that peace has come, how can one help recognizing the freedom that has occurred as the Word of God made flesh? We have seen the loaves and fishes multiplied, sufficing and more than sufficing. Are we to deny those? Yes, as loaves and fishes. The most that we can let ourselves see and recognize is that all fulfillment is in God, and comes from God, and *is* God, and it matters not at all in what form it is seen. Our gratitude can never be for the loaves and fishes, but that we have been allowed to see and know the fulfillment that is God.

Once, it seemed so easy. In the beginning, there were promises that seemed to be fulfilled, needs that were answered. One thought it would continue in that way, growing better and better. But one cannot expect that the problems will ever vanish totally. As one advances spiritually, they may seem to intensify and to weigh more heavily. Is this a denial of what we were first promised? I think not. If we took that promise as one of an easier road, a road with less and less burdens, we had ignored everything we have ever read of the lives of spiritual men.

If and when we ever achieve the happy ending, with ourselves walking shining and free from chains to a blissful eternity, we shall have lost all sense of ourselves and humanity, and we shall have disappeared from the human scene. But while we live in the human scene, among men of varying degrees of consciousness, we shall find problems that we can grow free of only by an ever deepening, more intense knowledge of God. They will not be the same problems with which we were formerly faced. A grown-up is no longer troubled by the sicknesses and fears of childhood. The grown-up can do his fractions and his decimals now, but the problems of higher mathematics overtake him as his knowledge increases.

We must not ask nor seek for that human happy ending. More and more we must turn to God for

37

the forgetting of ourselves, for the sake of God only, for the realization of God not as A power, but as Power only; not as the Cause of an effect—not even as Cause *and* effect—but as all there is, with neither Cause nor effect considered. Cause and effect are of the human world, and our reach must be beyond that. We shall be dragged back to this world, to complain of it, or to be grateful for delivery from its troubles. And again and again we must reach forward beyond it.

It is a hard task that is before us, denying us everything we thought essential. No one can say whether the last deliverance will ever be known by any of us. I am in no way sure that it matters whether it will or not. It is the climbing of the mountain that matters, and not the ultimate view from its top. That view is an achievement we will be tempted to think of as having been made by us, or as having been granted by Grace. We should know by now that an achievement, of no matter how rarefied a stature, is never what we are seeking. To believe that a search must have an ending, and that it is useless without one, is to cling still to the material belief of struggle and fulfillment, of winning a final prize, a crown set upon one's head. And then one is back where one started, in the scale of values one was so desperately trying to leave. In the deepest sense of truth, we are already beyond it. We are fulfillment ourselves, and the harmony and security we are seeking are within ourselves. This is what we have always to know, always to remember. No one has ever said that it was easy.

(A Student.)

CHAPTER THREE

PROTECTION

IN the material sense of life, the word "protection" brings up the thought of defense or armor, a hiding place from an enemy, or some sense of withdrawal from danger. In the mental sciences, protection refers to some thought or idea, or some form of prayer that would save one from injury or hurt from an outside source. In the use of the word "protection" thought is immediately drawn to the fact that existing somewhere is a destructive or harmful activity or presence or power, and that protection, by word or thought, is a means of finding security from this danger to one's self or one's affairs.

In The Infinite Way we have learned that God is One: therefore, God is one power, and we live in that conscious One-ness. The moment the idea of God as One begins to dawn in consciousness we understand that in all this world there is no power and no presence from which we need protection. You will see this as you dwell on the word "Omnipresence," and realize that in this All-presence of Good you are completely alone with a divine harmony—a harmony which pervades and permeates consciousness, and is in itself the All-ness and the Only-ness of Good.

Ponder this idea and meditate upon it, and note how the revelation and assurance comes to you, within your own being, that this is true: there is but One, and because of the nature of that One there is no outside influence for either good or evil. There is no presence or power to which to pray for any good that does not already exist as Omnipresence, right where you are. In your periods of communion note the assurance that comes with the realization that God alone *is,* and that God's Presence is infinite. There is no other power; there is no other Presence; there is no destructive or harmful influence in any person, place or thing; there is no evil in any condition. God could not be One and yet find an existence separate and apart from that One. God alone is being—think of that, *God alone is Being.* How then can you pray to God in word or thought, or how can you defend yourself, mentally or physically, in the realization of God as being the One and the Only Being?

The Master has told us: "There is nothing from without a man, that entering into him can defile him: but the things which come out of him, those are they that defile the man." Our studies and meditations have revealed that whatever of discord or inharmony is manifest in our experience today is coming through the activity of *our own thought.* We have accepted the universal belief of a power, a presence and an activity apart from God; we have accepted the belief that some one or some thing, outside of our own being, can be a presence or power for evil in our experience; and the acceptance of this rather universal belief causes much of our discord and inharmony.

As we consciously bring ourselves back, day after

day, day after day, to the actual awareness of God as Infinite Being, God manifesting and expressing Itself as our individual being, we understand more fully that all power flows out from us, through us, as a benediction and blessing to the world, but that *no power acts upon us from without our own being*. As students of The Infinite Way, it must become clear to us that there is no power acting upon us from without our own being for either good or evil. Just as we have learned that the stars, the creations of God in the heavens, cannot act upon us in accord with astrological belief, so we have learned that conditions of weather, climate, infection, contagion, or accident likewise cannot act injuriously upon those who have come into some measure, at least, of the understanding of the nature of God and the nature of individual being. We are constantly being reminded to become more and more aware of the nature of God, the nature of prayer, and the nature of individual being, so that we will understand ourselves as the off-spring of God, of whom it is truly said, "Son, thou art ever with me, and all that I have is thine."

All of human existence is made up of the belief of two powers—the good and the evil. All religion in its beginning was nothing more nor less than an attempt to find something to deliver us from external conditions or powers of evil. Even today most religions deal with a concept of God as being some kind of great Power which, if we can only reach It, will protect and save us from these destructive influences which, it is claimed, exist outside our own being.

Think seriously on this subject of protection or protective work, because each day we are faced with suggestions of impending or threatened dangers. Always some person, some place, or some thing is being presented as a great danger or destructive power which we must fear, or from which we must seek a God to save us. Of course, if there were such dangers, and if there were such a God, the world would have discovered, long before this, some way to reach that God.

God's All-ness makes it utterly impossible for any destructive or evil influence or power to exist anywhere—in heaven, on earth, or in hell—so do not make the mistake of thinking of God as some great power which is able to save you from a destructive person or influence if only you can reach Him. Do not make the common mistake of thinking that The Infinite Way is just another method of finding God, or another manner of praying to bring God's influence into your experience in order to overcome discord, error, evil, sin and disease. No! Rather, understand that this Message is bringing the awareness of God as One; of God as infinite individual being; of God as All-Presence and All-Power.

The universal belief in two powers, good and evil, will continue to operate in our experience until we individually—remember this, you and I individually—reject the belief of two powers. In the tenth chapter of Luke, you will read that the Master sent the seventy disciples out, "two by two, into every city and place, whither he himself would come." When the seventy returned they rejoiced, saying, "Lord, even the devils are subject unto us through thy name." But the Master replied, ". . . rejoice not, that the spirits are subject unto you: but rather rejoice, because your names are written in heaven."

In this age we need a great deal of protective thought, but the nature of that thought must be the realization that God's All-ness precludes the possibility of there ever existing a source of evil in the world itself, or one able to operate in individual experience. Our protective work, or our prayers for protection, must consist of the realization that nothing exists anywhere, at any time in our experience of the past, present or future, that is of a destructive nature. Through our studies and meditations eventually we will come to that God-contact within us, wherein we receive the divine assurance: "Lo, I am with you alway." This will not come as a protection against evil powers or destructive forces, but as a continuous assurance of One Presence, One Power, One Being, One Life, One Law. It is in this awareness of One-ness that we find our peace.

It would be a wonderful thing if students would take this subject of protection into daily meditation for the next month or two, saying nothing about it to anyone. Do not discuss or mention it, but just keep it a secret subject within yourselves until you arrive at a place in consciousness where you actually can feel that God is One, and that the secret of protection lies not in seeking a God to save or secure you against some outside intrusion, but rather that safety, security and peace are entirely dependent on your remembrance and realization of the truth of God as One—Infinite One.

Do you not see that the world is seeking peace (just as it is seeking safety and security) outside of its own being? Whereas, no peace, no safety and no security will ever be found except in our individual realization of God as One—the Only Being, Presence and Power. We cannot tell the world about peace or safety or security, but we can find it for ourselves and thereby let the world see by our experience that we have found a Way higher than superstitious belief in some power of good that miraculously saves us from some power of evil. We cannot tell the world that there is no danger from outside sources, influences or powers, but our realization of this truth can make the harmony and completeness and perfection of our lives so evident that others, one by one, will turn to seek that which we have found.

What *have* we found? Have we found a God to whom we can pray, and from whom we can receive special favors that others, less favored, cannot receive? Have we found a God to whom we can pray and receive healing or supply or protection? No! No! We have found no such thing: we have found God as One; *we have found God as our very being*. We have found God to be the Life—not a life subject to sin, disease or death, but the One and Only Life; we have found God to be eternal and immortal Life, our very individual life. We have found God to be the Law—not a law that can be used to offset laws of heredity, infection, contagion or disease, but the One Infinite, Omnipresent Law—maintaining and sustaining the harmony and perfection of Its own creation at all times.

God is One, and beside Him there is no other. Because we know the nature of God as One, we know the nature of prayer as the realization of One-ness.

"Look unto me and be ye saved, all the ends of the earth: for I am God, and there is none else."

(Isa. 45:22.)

Spiritual Reliance

Spiritual harmony comes quickly when we have given up the desire or search for physical, or outer harmony. This is the inner meaning of the Master's words: "Peace I leave with you, my peace I give unto you: not as the world giveth, give I unto you." Divine Grace comes in proportion as we turn from all sense of human peace, prosperity or health, and seek the realization of "My Peace," which includes the health or harmony of Spirit.

Paul tells us: "Be not deceived; God is not mocked: for whatsoever a man soweth, that shall he also reap. For he that soweth to his flesh shall of the flesh reap corruption; but he that soweth to the Spirit shall of the Spirit reap life everlasting." We must understand that in the first case we are being warned against a faith, confidence, reliance or dependence on the creature—that is, that which appears as effect. However, to "sow to the Spirit," by placing one's reliance and trust and hope in the Infinite Invisible is to reap the things of the Spirit, and in this way we honor the Creator rather than the creature. This is what the prophet Isaiah meant when he warned the Hebrews against their faith in ". . . the work of their own hands, that which their own fingers have made," and a deep principle is revealed in this warning.

At this point of our unfoldment it is necessary to realize that we have left behind the Law of Moses, and that we have stepped out into the Grace of Truth. Surely by now we know that good humans are not rewarded by God, nor are bad humans punished by God. Whatever of reward or punishment comes into human experience comes through our own belief in such. Too often students complain bitterly about the problems they experience while on their search for God, not realizing how fortunate they are to be in the midst of these problems while seeking the revelation and realization of God, because until one has been divested of every human or material aid one cannot know the experience of a complete reliance on the Infinite Invisible.

We are born into a world where first we learn to rely on parents, later on teachers, husbands or wives, and often we end up dependent upon our children. In between we become dependent upon medicines and dollars, so that at no time in the average person's experience does he ever learn that there is an Infinite Invisible which is far better able to supply his every need, and far more dependable than any one or any thing in the visible realm. For the human, content to go through life in this way, it is naturally pleasurable to find at hand those people and things upon which he can rely, but fortunate is he if he does not come to the end of his rope and find that humans and material resources have failed him.

However, those who have set themselves on the search for God will find their journey shortened by every experience of failure on the part of friends and relatives and things, because then comes the complete reliance on that which has heretofore never been experienced—the Infinite Invisible. And what spiritual treasures we can bring forth through the realization to be gained from: "My grace is sufficient for thee," and "Man shall not live by bread alone, but by every word that proceedeth out of the mouth of God."

An Important Point in Spiritual Practice

Spiritual practice, which embraces all phases of the healing work, is much more than declaring or knowing some truth after a discord has been brought to your attention. Spiritual practice is a constant, conscious realization of God as Omnipresence—of God as the Life, Law, Substance, continuity, activity, the very Soul and intelligence of *all* being.

Suppose at this very moment you were to receive a call asking for help, and you proceed to give a treatment, to pray, or to go into meditation or communion. If, consciously or unconsciously, you have accepted the discord, and expect and hope that harmony is going to be restored through your treatment or prayer your success will be very limited, and your failures will be more numerous than your successes.

When a call comes announcing some form of discord it is necessary to remember consciously that this is not a discord or maladjustment which, through your effort or even through God, is to be corrected, but rather that this is a specific call to know that as God was in the beginning, so God is *now*, and God ever will be!

Unless you are living the spiritual life in such a manner as keeps you in the realization that the past and the future are *one*—here and now in the present—you will find yourself in distress if a call comes saying, "My friend has just been killed: please help me." You will be in a very embarrassing position indeed, because you will be expected either to raise the dead or to accept death as an actual happening, and merely give a treatment or meditation for the comfort of the bereft one. This situation must never come to you: you must never be in such a state of consciousness where anyone can announce that someone has been killed or has passed on, and then from that point expect to do something spiritual about it.

In living the true spiritual life you are not waiting for calls of discord and inharmony. You are living in such a state of consciousness that *God alone is the reality*, and your entire experience is one of dwelling in the realization of God ever governing, maintaining and sustaining Its own universe—from the beginning of time until the end of the world.

"Before Abraham was, I am. I am with you alway, even unto the end of the world." This brings that past and the future into the present: if *I am* with you since before Abraham, nothing could have occurred before that call except that which was a part of the demonstration of *I am*—the all-inclusive Love, Presence and Power of God. If *I am* with you until the end of the world, nothing can happen today, tomorrow or next week which is not a part of the all-embracing guidance, direction and protection of the divine principle of this universe.

48

In ordinary metaphysical practice, consciously or unconsciously you accept the fact that there are those in the world who are suffering from discord and inharmony, and that at any moment someone may telephone or come in person asking for help, and if you are not very, very careful you will be tempted to give it. Unless you are already living in the consciousness of God as the omnipresent Law and Being, the omnipresent Good, the omnipresent direction, guidance, intelligence, wisdom, substance and reality, you will automatically attempt, through spiritual means, to bring about adjustments, healings, harmonies and resurrections, all based on the fact that a sin or disease, accident or death have already occurred.

The Infinite Way is not a practice that begins with a call for help. The Infinite Way is a way of life in which, at all times, we live and move and have our being in the realization of God as Omnipresence, and in that consciousness, whenever an appearance or call of discord reaches us, we are enabled to smile in the true knowledge that no discord or inharmony has ever happened, therefore is not now in need of adjustment.

Here is one of the most important points to be achieved on the Spiritual Path. At one time I was taught that practitioners should consciously and specifically know the truth every day: that all who needed me would find me. It took only twenty-four hours to learn that this was a denial of the Christ. How could I, in one breath, say, "Those who need me will find me," and in the next, when they came to me, say, "God governs you; God is your life;

You are perfect now"? Do you not see that it is up to us to know, before anyone comes to us, that perfection *was* the true state of their being, and that perfection *is* the true state of their being in the here and now? Do you really believe that we have anything to do with establishing or bringing about harmony? No! No! Our place in the Spiritual Path is not to be repairers of damage nor resurrectors of life, nor physicians nor protective influences—that is God's function! And not only now, but from the beginning it has been God's function to be the creative principle of this universe, and to be the maintaining and sustaining principle *unto all time.*

If you understand the nature of God you will understand that God is the creative principle of all existence; God is the law unto all creation; God is the substance, the reality and the continuity of all creation. Therefore, all creation is in and of God, subject to God's government and God's care. It is your function to know this truth. Ye shall know this truth, and this truth will make you free—free of accepting appearances and then trying to do something about them.

Do you see wherein the Message of The Infinite Way, and its practice, differs from the greater part of metaphysical teachings? Living the Infinite Way means living in the constant, conscious realization of God as Infinite, Omnipresent, Eternal Being. It means living always in the consciousness that before Abraham was, *I am* the divine principle, the protective, maintaining and sustaining influence unto this universe. It also means living in the constant, conscious realization of the truth that *I am* with you unto the end of the world, and just as nothing could happen to you yesterday, so nothing could happen to you today or tomorrow, except as a part of God's Grace.

We could live lives of constant miracles if only we would abide in the consciousness of this truth: "My grace is sufficient for thee." Thy Grace is sufficient for every need, but not Thy Grace that is coming tomorrow. Thy Grace, since before Abraham was, is my sufficiency; Thy Grace is my sufficiency unto the end of the world. Thy Grace of the past, present and future *is at this very instant my sufficiency in all things*. Every day there are temptations to believe that we or our families or students are in need of something in the nature of form (it may be food, housing, opportunity, education, employment, rest) but to all those things we can respond: "Man shall not live by bread alone, but by every word that proceedeth out of the mouth of God," because Thy Grace is man's sufficiency in every instance.

From these two scriptural passages you can build such a consciousness of the omnipresence of the Infinite Invisible that forever after you will learn to love and enjoy and appreciate everything in the world of form and everything that exists as effect, yet never have the feeling that you need or require *anything*. Since God's Grace is your sufficiency you do not live by effect alone, but by every Word of Truth that has been embodied in your consciousness, and by every passage of Truth that you have made your own.

Affirming truths and denying errors will not make your demonstration. You must *learn to live by every word of truth,* and make every Word of Truth a part of your consciousness so that it becomes flesh of your flesh, bone of your bone, until the past, present and future are all bound up in the conscious realization of *God's Grace* as your sufficiency. In other words, your consciousness of Truth is the source and substance and activity and law of your daily demonstration of Good.

To those who are accepting the Message of The Infinite Way as a way of life, I would like to sum this up by asking that you go back and bring your past into your present by spending some time during this next month consciously realizing that God's Grace was your sufficiency in what you call your past; and that since before Abraham was, God's government of this universe has been so perfect that nothing of a discordant or inharmonious nature can happen to you or to anyone else, today or tomorrow. And so, should you hear of a sin, a disease, an accident or a death, immediately realize that it could not have happened, since from the beginning of time God has been the only law and reality unto His universe. Then you will know the true meaning of spiritual healing. You will know what Christ-consciousness is; you will know what it means to live and move and have your being in God-consciousness, never accepting appearances, temptations, discords, sins, diseases or accidents as anything other than temptations to believe in time and space.

If you are able to see that the past must become the present so that you are able to cover it all with the term *I am, I am* with you, *I am* with you in the past, *I am* with you in the present, *I am* with you since before Abraham was, *I am is* the law unto you, has been the law unto you, you will be able to take the next step and bring the future right down to the present, so that "unto the end of the world" will be embraced in your consciousness the consciousness of the Omnipresence of *I am*. In this way your whole universe will be embraced in the time and space since before Abraham *was*, unto the end of the world—all of it brought down to the here and now of *I am with you*.

The only time is God's time—*now*. God's time has existed since before Abraham *was*, and will continue to exist until the end of the world. Because *I am* with you since before Abraham was and unto the end of the world, *I am* is the immediate present —*now*. God's Grace *now* is your sufficiency, and the sufficiency unto your family and friends and students—and unto all who can accept God's Grace.

Punishment

Sometimes secrets, so deep and so profound, are revealed to us that we are shaken from head to foot, and when this happens we learn something not only new, but something that must make a drastic change in our lives. Such is the experience when we realize the nature of punishment and the reasons for punishment in our experience.

To understand that God neither rewards nor punishes is an important step in your spiritual development. If you have been at all impressed with this statement, you have pondered and meditated upon it, and somewhere along this line of inner reflection you have come to the realization that all of the religious theories which have been taught on the subject of punishment have been erroneous, and this itself should have made a startling change in your life. If you have the courage to continue your inner cogitation along this line, ultimately you will be led to the truth about punishment and the reason for punishment, and this will give you the opportunity to remold your life.

God is individual being, which means that God is the only Self, and there is no way for any hurt or evil to enter to defile the infinite purity of the Soul of God, nor anything at which evil can strike or attach itself. God is the Self of you, therefore God is the Self of me, and if I were in any way to hurt or offend you, to whom is my offence directed but to myself? This clarifies the Master's words: "Inasmuch as ye have done it unto one of the least of these my brethren, ye have done it unto me:" and with this understanding you begin to see that every bit of good done by you at any time in your entire life has been a good done to, for, and within yourself; and you also begin to see that every evil or thought of evil you have ever directed toward another, every lie and evasion of truth has been directed toward your own self, and therefore *the punishment is inflicted upon you by you*, because your act or thought of deceit, supposedly directed toward another, was actually directed toward yourself.

When the Master repeated the age-old wisdom: "Wherefore all things whatsoever ye would that men should do to you, do ye even so to them: for this is the law and the prophets;" He was giving us a principle: unless we do unto others as we would have others do unto us, we injure not the others but ourselves. In this present state of human consciousness it is true that the evil thoughts and dishonest acts and thoughtless words that we send out to others do harm them temporarily, but in the end always it will be found that the injury was not nearly so much to them as it was to ourselves.

In the days to come, when men recognize the great truth that God is the Selfhood of each individual, the evil aimed at us from another will never touch us, but will immediately rebound upon the one who sends it. In the degree that we recognize God as our individual being, we also realize that no weapon that is formed against us can prosper, since the only "I", the only "Me", is God, and we will not fear what man can do to us, since the Selfhood of us is God and cannot be harmed, and our realization of this will quickly send back the evil, and much more quickly than has heretofore been the case.

Once the first realization of this truth comes to us we understand that there is no longer any use concerning ourselves with what our neighbor does unto us, but looming large in our consciousness will be the realization that we must watch ourselves— morning, noon and night we must watch our thoughts, our words, our actions, to see that we ourselves do not send out anything of a negative nature which would be bound to have its result within our own being.

Never for a moment believe that this will result in your being good in order to avoid punishment.

This revelation goes far deeper than that: it enables you to see that God is your Selfhood, and that anything of an erroneous or negative nature that emanates from any individual is given power only in the degree that you yourself give it power. In your meditation it will result in the revelation of the nature of your true being—of God as the nature of your Life and Soul, and in that realization you will see that this is the truth of *all* men, and that the only way and mode of successful living is to understand your neighbor to be yourself.

And so it is that whatever of good or of evil you do unto others, you do unto the Christ of your own being—"Inasmuch as ye have done it unto one of the least of these my brethren, ye have done it unto me."

Why?

When help is asked on certain physical or mental conditions, the question is often asked: Why is the so-called spiritual healing only a partial healing, and why sometimes is it never a complete healing? Also, why is it that a person about to undergo surgery asks for help and receives a miraculous healing, although not one that precludes the necessity for surgery? Why is it that the patient undergoing surgery is kept entirely free of infection or after-effect and makes a more rapid recovery than would normally be the case, and yet, if God has anything to do with that much of the healing, why did not God make the surgery unnecessary?

First of all, you must understand that there are no degrees of Truth. Truth is absolute. God is absolute.

God is absolute Truth; God is absolute Being; God is infinite, eternal, immortal, omnipresent perfection. *God is all.* Therefore, the all-ness in the infinity and completeness and perfection of God being established, any measure less than that, experienced by the patient, represents the conditioned state of consciousness which makes it impossible to bring through or realize the completeness of the activity of God.

Here you have two factors: the consciousness of the practitioner and the consciousness of the patient. Let us assume that the consciousness of the practitioner is far higher and deeper than that of the patient, and so the patient comes to the practitioner with a conditioned state of consciousness in which it is not possible for him to open his consciousness completely to the fullness of the activity of God. It may be that there is so much attachment to the body and to the sense of personal health that the patient does not completely let go, and thus receive the full benefit of the infinite completeness and perfection of the activity of God as individual consciousness. Although the practitioner may be an instrument for a complete and perfect healing, the conditioned consciousness of the patient does not always allow this to come through.

On the other hand, the practitioner may not be up to the experience of the miracle of complete healing. To be in the highest state of consciousness, the practitioner has reached that elevation of spiritual awareness in which no effort is ever made to contact God for the purpose of healing. He is abiding in the consciousness of God as individual being, hence in the realization that the individual is already at the standpoint of immortality and eternality, that state of being to which nothing can be added.

The practitioner who is trying to use Truth over error, who is contacting God for the purpose of establishing harmony, or who is still in the third dimension of life, in which body is something separate and apart from spiritual consciousness, will make the mistake of being concerned with health as against disease, or will permit himself to be concerned with what appears to be something less than perfection in the visible scene.

For perfect healing the practitioner must abide in the consciousness of *God as the infinite all,* which means abiding in the fourth dimension of life in which no recognition is given to the pairs of opposites—good and evil, rich and poor, moral and immoral, immortal and mortal. In this fourth dimensional consciousness, or Christ-consciousness, the practitioner is never aware of someone or something to be healed or corrected, but is always aware of the Omnipresence of God's Being.

When the practitioner is able to abide in Christ-consciousness and have always "that mind which was also in Christ Jesus", then the fullness of God's Being freely flows, and regardless of whether it is an acute illness or a chronic one, or whether the illness is at the point of surgery, the practitioner can bring to conscious realization and demonstration the complete healing or unfoldment of divine harmony. When the practitioner's consciousness is at all conditioned, then the healing can only come through in proportion to the degree of conditioning of the practitioner's consciousness. In order to complete the experience of instantaneous or complete healing, the patient also must approach this work without the conditioned thought of believing that the power of God can bring one through illness, even though not able to perform the entire unfoldment of harmony without the aid of surgery. At least, the patient should be able to relax with no preconceived thought or opinion as to what will take place, and *let* the divine consciousness of the practitioner have full sway.

You can readily see that the main responsibility rests with the practitioner. When the practitioner truly rises above the pairs of opposites to that state of consciousness in which all sense of both health and disease are absent, and when any phase of the human picture does not bring a reaction which has behind it the desire to heal, correct, save, renew or regenerate, then in that spiritually illumined state of consciousness the practitioner will bring through greater works.

As you approach that state of non-reaction to the world of appearances whereby you do not react happily to the good appearances, and certainly do not react fearfully or doubtfully to the evil appearances, you will do far greater healing works, and will be able to impart to those who come to you a greater confidence in the great Truth that *God is*, which means that harmony *is*, perfection *is*, reality *is*— and, in spite of all appearances to the contrary, *good alone is*.

CHAPTER FOUR

IMMORTALITY

THE most prevalent concept of immortality is an existence of eternal bliss after a point of transition known as death or passing on. Another popular concept of immortality is a Methuselah-plus existence in this world. Both concepts are incorrect. The first is based upon the faulty premise that death could be a part of God's Creation. The second is merely a gilded notion of longevity.

The only death, passing on, or transition is, in the words of Paul, "I die daily"—the transition from one state of consciousness to another. To "die daily" means simply to drop the limited, material concept for one more nearly spiritual. There is no loss of consciousness in this activity.

Sooner or later, each one on this spiritual Path comes to a place in his development where he realizes the impossibility of dying or passing on. The individual going through the period of transition is merely exchanging one state of consciousness for another—as a child does when he becomes a youth; a youth when he becomes an adult; and an adult upon entering maturity. All of these are differing states or planes of consciousness, yet no death or passing on has taken place: there is only transition from one state of consciousness to another.

At first this may sound strange, since it appears

that no one exists in our immediate presence more than, at most, one hundred to one hundred and ten years. So it would seem that, with the exception of a few reputed to have remained on earth for three or four hundred years, everyone, sooner or later, must experience death, pasing on, or transition. This, however, is not true.

It is true that, at some period or other, we all pass from human sight. However, in the experience of those who pass from human sight, there is no body left for burial or cremation. That picture remains only to those still on the material plane of consciousness. Those who are more highly illumined understand that body and individuality are inseparable.

Throughout The Infinite Way Writings and in our class-work, it has been stated that no one has ever died. From the beginning of time, no one has ever died, and no one ever will. No one has ever passed on; no one has ever experienced death by passing on. The experience of death, or passing on, is one that takes place only in the consciousness of those who are left behind: that is, those who still entertain this belief of death or passing on.

It follows, as a natural, logical progression, that in all the world there is no disease, and there is no old age. Without disease and old age, there can be no death. Therefore, since Life is eternal, there cannot be disease, old age or death.

The second concept of immortality, that of remaining on earth for one hundred, two hundred, or five hundred years, is nothing more than a concept of longevity. Longevity is not immortality: it is merely a continuation of the present physical sense of existence.

The understanding of immortality is the realization of one's God-being, God-identity, God-consciousness. This permits one to develop naturally and gently from infancy to adulthood, from adulthood to maturity, and from maturity to whatever planes of consciousness are necessary for spiritual unfoldment and development, and whatever work God has in store.

An interesting substantiation for this subject is to be found in the Apocryphal book, "The Wisdom of Solomon" (1:12-15): "Court not death in the error of your life: Neither draw upon yourselves destruction by the works of your hands: Because God made not death; Neither delighteth he when the living perish: For he created all things that they might have being: And the generative powers of the world are healthsome, And there is no poison of destruction in them: Nor hath Hades (the kingdom of death) royal dominion upon earth, For righteousness is immortal."

Notice this last statement: "And the generative powers of the world are healthsome, and there is no poison of destruction in them: nor hath Hades (death) royal dominion upon earth." There is no kingdom of death upon the earth, and the reason given is: "For righteousness is immortal." As we ponder this, beginning with God and following out from God, we can find nothing of death, nothing of the poison of destruction, nothing of unhealthiness, nothing of the kingdom of Hades upon the earth.

In the second chapter of this same Apocryphal book, verse 23, we read: "Because God created man for incorruption, And made him an image of his own proper being." If God created man to be immortal, there is no presence or power able to thwart the Will of God. If God made man to be "an image of his own proper being," there is no presence or power in this entire universe that could end that Being. When these points are grasped, we begin to understand the impossibility of death for anyone. Once we accept God as the creative Principle of the universe, we see the absurdity of "the poison of destruction," or the kingdom of death upon the earth.

Be assured of this: God has a spiritual work for each of us, and we have God-capacity to perform it. In the realization of this truth, we will no longer think of longevity as immortality; we will not be concerned with the visible span of our years on earth, but rather with the demonstration of our eternal Selfhood, forever about the Father's business.

*   *   *

"And Moses was an hundred and twenty years old when he died: his eye was not dim, nor his natural force abated."

(Deut. 34:7.)

"But they that wait upon the Lord shall renew their strength; they shall mount up with wings as eagles; they shall run, and not be weary; and they shall walk, and not faint."

(Isa. 40:31.)

"Bless the Lord, O my soul. . . . Who satisfieth

thy mouth with good things; so that thy youth is renewed like the eagles.

(Ps. 103: see 1-5.)

"Grow old along with me!
The best is yet to be,
The last of life,
For which the first was made:
Our times are in His hand
Who saith, 'A whole I planned,
Youth shows but half;
Trust God: see all, nor be afraid.' "
(Rabbi Ben Ezra: Robert Browning.)

When an old and beloved friend has passed, the question is often asked: What can be done now and in the future?

Is there a God? If there *is* a God, not even a sparrow falls. If there *is* a God, life is continuous and progressive: the passing from this plane of existence is merely a passing from one of the many mansions into another of the many mansions. If there *is* a God, there is no such thing as death, and if there is no death, why mourn those who pass from our human sight?

Each, in his time, will leave this plane of consciousness. Those in ignorance of God may be forced out of their bodies by disease or old age. Those with some acquaintanceship with God will make the transition without the necessity of death, discord or infirmities, but all eventually will leave this plane, and the reason is this: as we pass from infancy to childhood, a delightful state of consciousness, we leave one of God's mansions and, with growing pains, we pass into adulthood. There are two ways to make the transition from childhood into maturity, and one is the looking-back process, trying to re-live the days of the past. The other way is to realize that the transition from infancy to childhood and from childhood into adulthood is an activity of God, and those who accept that do not experience the infirmities of old age.

Battling the advancing years as if they were an evil is what produces the discords in our experience. Opening consciousness to the normal, natural transition from one state of adulthood to another will enable us to look forward to the experience of the middle years and the advanced years.

The Master said, ". . . this is life eternal, that they might know thee, the only true God. . . ." In other words, God Life is individual life, your life and mine. That statement is made again and again in all spiritual teachings, and if it were accepted literally, all ageing processes would cease. The Life of God cannot age! The Life of God is not receptive to a calendar! We give power to the calendar, but the body cannot. The body has no intelligence with which to know what year it is, and if we accept the calendar it operates through our bodies and through our minds, and appears on the body and makes its manifestations there. Since the calendar, in and of itself, has no power, and our bodies, in and of themselves, have no power, it must be we, ourselves, who give power to the calendar to age us, because the only thing that can act upon us is what we accept in consciousness.

Immortality means your individual immortality, here and now, which would include the immortality of your being and of your body. So let it be agreed in your consciousness that God is Life, but more than that, *God is your life!*

"Even every one that is called by my name: for I have created him for my glory, I have formed him; yea, I have made him."

(Isa. 43:7.)

"For I have no pleasure in the death of him that dieth, saith the Lord God; wherefore turn yourselves, and live ye."

(Ezek. 18:32.)

"Thou art worthy, O Lord, to receive glory and honour and power: for thou hast created all things, and for thy pleasure they are and were created."

(Rev. 4:11.)

These scriptural passages clearly indicate that God created us for his own pleasure, and this is an eternal relationship. And so, as we witness ourselves and our friends advancing into more mature years, let us realize our function as an infant and as a child, as an adult, and see how progressive each step has been, and then look forward to the revelation of what the future years have in store through the Grace of God. Then, as we watch our friends pass from sight, let us rejoice that they have passed from one mansion into another. They have not died because of sin, because God never punishes sin. God is a God of love and forgiveness "until seventy times seven."

Our transition is for the glory of God, and for the glory of the development of our individual Soul, and those of us who are approaching the middle years and beyond the middle years must learn to ask the Father, "What have you now for me to do?" Then, as other experiences come, open your vision and realize that just as the flowers bloom and seem to fade and then bloom again, so do we pass through many transitional experiences, but death is never known in any of these experiences.

Death is our interpretation of what we are witnessing, but it is an observation based on ignorance. Those who have caught the first tiny glimpse of God understand that God is Life, and that God is Life Eternal—life without death, "for he is thy life, and the length of thy days." This can only come as you lift your vision above selfishness, above limitations, above the desire to hold others in bondage to form. The worm must emerge from its cocoon in order to become a butterfly. Everyone and everything passes through transitional states and, through spiritual evolution and development, each one ultimately finds himself sitting at the foot of the Throne, returned to the Father's House.

The Price of Truth

"Again, the kingdom of heaven is like unto treasure hid in a field; the which when a man hath found, he hideth, and for joy thereof goeth and selleth all that he hath, and buyeth that field."

(Matt. 13:44.)

The Roman poet, Ovid, once said: "The most acceptable gifts always are those which the giver makes precious," and if this be so, no gift could be more precious or more appreciated than Truth. Truth bears a tremendous price. Truth cannot be bought for spare change, or in your spare time. There is no way of acquiring or demonstrating Truth unless you are willing to sell *all* you have to buy it.

After studying Truth for twenty or thirty years, many people wonder why they do not seem much better off than before, and this is due, primarily, to the fact that they have accepted the teachings of the Master only in part. Many affirm that the entire Truth teaching is to be found in the teachings of Jesus, but how many have seriously studied the views of Jesus on the point of how much we must pay for Truth, and how much we must be prepared to sacrifice and relinquish?

In the days of old, one price was paid for this Truth—the human sense of life. Jesus paid that price. Peter, Paul, and John paid it, as did thousands of others who knew in advance that in turning to Truth they were risking loss of their human sense of life. Today, modern teachers of Truth are doing the same thing. In explaining that the Mind of God is your mind they are risking the displeasure of the entire human world. What they actually mean is that God is your individual mind, and that all the power of the Godhead is embodied in your individual mind.

The reason we do not always give outward evidence of this Truth is because we have not seriously accepted the Truth that God is our mind, and so we feel limited in many, many ways. For instance, if your telephone rang several times within an hour, with people asking for help, saying they were very sick, some of them dying, the chances are that about eighty per cent of you would say, "I am not qualified to give such help: you had better call a practitioner." You have been told that God is your mind, but you have not accepted that Truth as a fact. Therefore, you feel that there is a limitation to your healing power, whereas it is not *your* power at all. *It is the Mind of God that heals!* It was not Jesus' personal mind, nor His educated mind—it was the God-mind operating as the individual mind of Christ Jesus that did the healing work. *Let that Mind be in you!*

How can you let that Mind be in you except by *acknowledging that it is in you*? It is not a Mind separate and apart from you that you can admit *into* your mind. You can only let that Mind be your mind by the acknowledgment, "Thank you, Father, Thy Mind is my mind." Then when you are called upon for help of any nature you can say, "Certainly, I will help you." And you will have healings. The Master always said, "I can of mine own self do nothing," but the Mind that was in Christ Jesus (the Mind of God) fed five thousand, healed the multitudes, and raised the dead.

No demand can be made upon us that we cannot fulfill! Granted, we do not fulfill them all: we fail in some, but the sole reason is that we do not fully acknowledge that *God is our mind*. We accept it with certain limitations. We cajole ourselves with the thought that another year or two of study may do it for us, but this is not so. Only one thing makes the Law effective unto you and that is the acknowledgment that the Mind of God is your mind, and therefore your mind is fully capable of meeting any need, be it physical, mental, moral, or financial. Every need of human life that directs itself to you can be met through the Mind of Christ Jesus, which is your individual mind. God is no respecter of persons, therefore anything that is true of one is true of all. Jesus said, ". . . my Father and your Father"—your mind and my mind, and you can accept that literally.

Any healing that Jesus accomplished was through the same Mind which is in you. This is not egotism, nor is it boasting of personal power. This is the deepest humility in the world—humility which has no sanctimoniousness about it. This is the humility that acknowledges, "All power is given unto me by virtue of the fact that the Mind of Christ Jesus is my individual mind, and It can do all things."

Based on the Master's revelation that God is your individual mind, you can understand that there is no limit to your intelligence or your power. Then follow through to the realization that God is your life, and you will understand why you are immortal. As Jesus might have expressed it, "God is Life Eternal." You must then agree that Life has no ageing process, no changing process, and no death process. In the entire Plan of Life God has not provided one single death. If you were to thoroughly study the four Gospels you would find that the experience of death was never accepted by the Master as necessary and right, or just and natural. Whenever it was presented to Him, He overcame the appearance of death, but He could not have overcome it if death had been a reality. Never can a Law of God be set aside: two times two are four! If death were a Law, the Master never could have set it aside. Because God is individual life, the realization of that truth will make you free of every experience of physical inharmony, old age, or death.

It is not enough to hear these words, or to read them. There is a price to be paid. There was a time when you could not have purchased these truths from a spiritual master for thousands of dollars—they were considered too sacred, too secret, too precious. Today they are available to everyone in a ten-cent pamphlet. Perhaps it is because of this that we will not pay the real price—*that of application*, putting the Truth to work by accepting it as our consciousness.

When you realize that God is your mind, you have a treatment that should be in operation not less than a hundred times each day. Every time there is a temptation to believe in forgetfulness, *that* should be a constant reminder to realize God as individual mind, not by making affirmations about it, but by *knowing* the Truth, *remembering* the Truth—*realizing* that God is Mind, and It is capable of every demand made upon It.

This realization is a spiritual weapon which, if used, will protect you from bombs and wars. God is your life, and what can destroy the Life of God? You have no life to lose or to gain; you have no life to be healed or to die. There is only *one life*,

71

and that is the Life of God! The cause of all sin, all disease, all lack and limitation, old age and death is the belief and acceptance that we have a life of our own which had a beginning and which must have an ending. We have no such life!

Throughout all ages, and thousands of years before Christ, the revelation has been given that God is Life—individual life. The price we must pay for this Truth is the cultivation of the ability to discipline ourselves. Every time a suggestion comes that we have a limited life or a limited mind, we must constantly and consciously realize: "Since God is the Life of me, It can fulfill every demand made upon It. Since God is the Life of me, I am eternal, immortal, indestructible."

For all the glorious Gifts of God, the great price is *self-discipline*. Each of us has the right to accept these Gifts *in proportion* to the degree to which we develop our ability to discipline ourselves. *This is the price of truth!*

The Prayer

"Open my mind to righteous judgment,
Open my eyes to see the Christ in all I meet,
Open my ears to hear the Voice of God.
Open my mouth to speak the Word of Truth,
Open my heart to Love,
Open my hands to serve.
Guide my feet that I may walk in the path of
    whatever of Truth is unfolded to me and
    through me.
Thank you, Father."

(A Student.)

"Inasmuch as ye have done it unto one of the least of these my brethren, ye have done it unto me."

(Matt. 25:40.)

I have Overcome the World

"These things I have spoken unto you, that in me ye might have peace. In the world ye shall have tribulation; but be of good cheer; I have overcome the world."

(John 16:33.)

As you know, the Master wasted no words, and every statement He made must be considered in the light of a world shattering revelation. Every word must be considered as a truth, the understanding of which is vital to your individual experience. Upon reading these words of the Master, your first inclination might be to believe that He has overcome something external to His own state of consciousness: perhaps you might think that He has overcome people, lack, limitation, or war. It is possible that you may never have considered what the Master really meant when He said, "I have overcome the world," and in that case this is a good opportunity for meditation and reflection on this tremendous revelation.

The world is within you, and within me. There is no world outside of you or of me. The world exists nowhere except within the consciousness of the individual. The world is embodied within consciousness, and it appears to us as thought, and as our thought about the world. And so it is that our world is constituted either of a consciousness of Truth, or a series of universal beliefs which we entertain about the world. These beliefs may be somewhere near the correct understanding, or they may be far from it.

As humans, our world is made up of concepts of that which we behold, and of those people and things of which we become aware in the ordinary course of existence. It is for this reason that our world consists of love and hate; of confidence and fear; of health and disease; of riches and poverty; of sin and purity. The world which we entertain in thought is made up of two powers—good and evil. We love and desire that which we accept as good; we hate and fear that which we consider evil.

Our world consists of people, some of whom we like and trust, and others whom we do not like and in whom we have no confidence. We go to extremes of loving some and hating others. Our world is made up of concepts and our reactions to these concepts. It is this world which the Master said He had overcome, and, indeed, He had overcome the world of human beliefs, material concepts, theories and opinions.

"And Jesus being full of the Holy Ghost returned from Jordan, and was led by the Spirit into the wilderness, being forty days tempted of the devil. And in those days he did eat nothing: and when they were ended, he afterward hungered. And the devil said unto him, If thou be the Son of God, command this stone that it be made bread. And Jesus answered him, saying, It is written, That man shall not live by bread alone, but by every word of God.

"And the devil, taking him up into an high mountain, shewed unto him all the kingdoms of the world in a moment of time. And the devil said unto him, All this power will I give thee, and the glory of them: for that is delivered unto me; and to whomsoever I will give it. If thou therefore wilt worship me, all shall be thine. And Jesus answered and said unto him, Get thee behind me, Satan: for it is written, Thou shalt worship the Lord thy God, and him only shalt thou serve.

And he brought him to Jerusalem, and set him on a pinnacle of the temple, and said unto him, If thou be the Son of God, cast thyself down from hence: for it is written, He shall give his angels charge over thee, to keep thee: And in their hands they shall bear thee up, lest at any time thou dash thy foot against a stone. And Jesus answering said unto him, It is said, Thou shalt not tempt the Lord thy God.

"And when the devil had ended all the temptation, he departed from him for a season."

(Luke 4:1-13.)

Each of these temptations, in its turn, had to be met within the thought of the Master, and pondered and wrestled within His own consciousness until He had overcome them. You will note that it is written, "And when the devil had ended all the temptation, he departed from him for a season," and by this we gather that there were recurring experiences of temptation in the life of the Master.

When the Master met with the multitudes he had

75

to overcome, within Himself, the universal belief of sickness and death, lack, danger—the belief in conditions and activities outside the government and control of God. These temptations were met and overcome in proportion to His complete reliance on the understanding that the government of His universe was upon the shoulders of "The Father within *Me*."

These temptations of the world appeared to the Master as if they were outside of His own being. They appeared as people undergoing disease and death, lack and limitation; as men who were sinful; as men who were betrayers and who were false to their trust. All temptations appear to us in this way. Never do we stop to realize that these appearances that touch our lives are not something *external* to us. We accept the appearance as if it were something outside our own consciousness, and our effort is to make the correction, improvement, or healing outside our own consciousness.

One of the high points of the Message of The Infinite Way reveals that although *appearances* may testify to the fact that there are evils outside our own being (that is, evils connected with people and conditions), we, as students, must immediately recognize that we are being tempted to believe that these are external people or conditions. We must realize that we are being tempted to do something to, for, or about them: whereas, all of this is taking place *within our own consciousness*, and must be met there.

If there are sick and sinful people in your experience, this temptation must be met within yourself until you come to the realization of God as individual being. If there are thieves in your world, meet this, too, as a temptation to accept the testimony of the senses. If there is lack and limitation in your experience, wrestle with the tempter within you until you come to that point of realization wherein it becomes clear that God is the Selfhood of individual being; that God constitutes *all* being.

As you overcome temptations within yourself, you overcome those phases of the world represented by such temptations. As you meet each temptation as it comes along, you too will reach that place in consciousness where you will be able to say, "I have overcome the world." And until then, even if you overcome it in a measure and by degrees, you will have been achieving harmony in your experience.

CHAPTER FIVE

THE COMFORTER

"Know ye not that ye are the temple of God, and that the Spirit of God dwelleth in you?"

(1 Cor. 3:16.)

THE time is approaching when the world will be so filled with the conscious realization of the Presence of God that all evil or error will be dispelled by the very presence of man.

The great secret of life is this: God is incarnated in man. God is manifest as man. God is in the midst of *you*—". . . the place where thou standest is holy ground." There is just as much of God in you, right where you are, as there would be if the heavens could open and God Itself come into you. If this were not true Jesus could not have healed, neither could the disciples nor the apostles, nor the metaphysical and spiritual practitioners of this day. You are divine, because the Spirit of God is manifest as your very being. God has embodied Itself as your Soul, Mind and Spirit. God, in Its essence, is invisible, God, in Its expression, is visible as you and as me.

In the days of old the Hebrews thought the Messiah was a man, but the One whom they thought was the Messiah said, "Before Abraham was, I am." Messiah is the Spirit of God in man, and the Hebrews who prophesied the coming of the Messiah were absolutely correct, except that they put it in time and space. The Messiah does not come in time and space: It comes in consciousness. The Christ, or Messiah, is born when you recognize the Presence of the Spirit of God in you. Never is this external: always it is within you, but the effect is external. Love goes before you and is felt by all whom you touch.

"But the Comforter, which is the Holy Ghost, whom the Father will send in my name, he shall teach you all things, and bring all things to your remembrance, whatsoever I have said unto you . . . I will send him unto you." The Comforter is your divine state of consciousness; that area of your consciousness which is the Christ, the Spirit of Truth the Savior, the Messiah. All of this is within you, and the moment you come near a person with the least degree of spiritual capacity, he knows it—he can feel it. Even an animal feels it. This is no part of your body or brain: it is the very consciousness of Truth Itself that is felt. The day will come when we will consciously be so full of the Presence of the Spirit of God that wherever we go our Christhood will be felt. The mere fact that our consciousness rests on an individual will be the healing touch. Wherever we go we will be a blessing and, even though not physically present, the remembrance or consciousness of us will be a healing influence.

This will be because of something that has taken place within our consciousness the moment we realize that we are the Christ, the Son of God, the very Spirit of God in expression. We will know this, however, only when we no longer fear or hate each other; when we no longer know envy, jealousy or malice of any kind. We cannot rid ourselves of these negative emotions, but the Christ can and does.

Human consciousness is made up entirely of wants and desires, and this you can sense whenever you come into the presence of one who, in any way, is wanting, desiring, hoping, competing, envying. On the other hand, Christ-consciousness brings with it every type of joy and abundant good, although not always according to the pattern of success or happiness that we, in our humanhood, have drawn. The things that we consider desirable might bring us great unhappiness and be our undoing. Many men have acquired and accomplished all the things their ambitions set out for them, and yet were unhappy and dissatisfied, and often ended in despair and destruction.

"I asked God for strength that I might achieve;
I was made weak that I might learn humbly to obey.
I asked for help that I might do greater things;
I was given infirmity that I might do better things.
I asked for riches that I might be happy;
I was given poverty that I might be wise.
I asked for power that I might have the praise of men;
I was given weakness that I might feel the need of God.
I asked for all things that I might enjoy life;
I was given life that I might enjoy all things.

I got nothing that I asked for, but everything
    that I had hoped for.
Almost despite myself my unspoken prayers
    were answered:
I am among all men most richly blessed."

The above wisdom was written by an anonymous
Confederate soldier, almost one hundred years ago.
And so it is that the Christ fulfills Itself in accord
with Its own idea of Love. "Love is the fulfilling of
the law." The Christ fulfills Itself in a change of
Spirit, and our human self is then so transformed
that we no longer recognize ourselves as we were.
When the comforter, the Spirit of God, comes to
consciousness there is no longer desire for things in
the outer realm, and we find there is nothing of a
human nature that needs fulfillment. Instead there
is only a spiritual sense, a desire or love for the
Spirit that insists on being inwardly fulfilled.

No one who has been touched by the Christ ever
again has any need to be concerned about supply,
be it money, friendship, companionship, love, home,
or any other type of supply. Even a tiny degree of
Christhood fulfills it, and the individual never again
has to take thought of what he shall eat, what he
shall drink, or wherewithal he shall be clothed. In-
stinctively this is felt whenever you come into the
presence of one who has attained even a measure of
the Christ, because there is nothing pulling on you,
no one trying to get something from you. The Christ
fulfills Itself without any need of turning to a person
or thing. Whatever comes (and it comes abundantly)
comes through the fulfilling of the law of Love.

Millions of people know how to pray—that is, they think they do. They know what they want, and if they cannot get it through ordinary human means they pray for it. Such prayer is sin, because it is desire. Not only is it desire, it is outlining what one thinks will be good for one. It is sin, because it is not relaxing and trusting that the Divine Consciousness knows our every need. When the Christ touches consciousness all things appear, all things happen, everything is taken care of.

Ultimately, when you understand the correct concept of prayer, you will understand that prayer is an inner resting in God; an inner conscious communion. And then you will understand why prayer has nothing to do with desire. Prayer has only to do with an awareness, a realization, a feeling of freedom, joy and peace. Each time you resist the temptation to pray for any thing, ask, wish, seek, or long for any thing, you are praying. You are acknowledging that God, the All-knowing Mind, already knows your needs, and you are acknowledging that the Love of God is your sufficiency. In the realization that you live and move and have your being in God, how could you pray for any thing? Even when temptation comes along and says you need this or that, Truth comes along and says, "God is fulfillment. God knoweth my need even before I do." When you have resisted the temptation to pray for things you have prayed aright, because you have communed with God. You have acknowledged Him in all thy ways. Then He will give thee rest.

When you are called upon for treatment, turn from the appearance and just reach out to God and let God give the treatment. Let God pray in you and through you. Let the Spirit of God bear witness with your spirit. Let the Spirit of God make intercession—you just be the listener and the beholder.

One Power

"Thus saith the Lord the King of Israel, and his redeemer the Lord of hosts; I am the first, and I am the last; and beside me there is no God."

(Isa. 44:6.)

Each time Truth has been presented to human consciousness it has gone through periods of progressive unfoldment, into organization, and through such organization has been lost again. There is one particular teaching that prevents men awakening to the truth of being. In the usual religious teaching there are two powers: the power of God and the power of the devil. The Power of God is good, and blesses; the power of the devil is evil, and damns. Always there are two powers; always God is battling the devil for your Soul; and always the question is, Who is going to win?

The only explanation for accidents, disasters, sickness, etc., is on the basis of two powers, or else making God responsible for the evils that happen to mankind. This latter, of course, cannot be true, for the simple reason that the specific message and mission of the Master was healing the sick and raising the dead, feeding the hungry and overcoming all the so-called natural disasters. In other words, the activity of the Christ is the answer and overcoming to all powers, so none of these things can possibly be the Will of God. In the Presence of God there is no evil.

Such teaching is much like the story of Job, wherein we find God permitting the devil to tempt one of His Children, and do all manner of evil to him. We know better than that: we know that in the Presence of God there is no devil and there is no evil. According to Genesis, "God saw every thing that he had made, and behold, it was very good." Therefore, if God made the devil, the devil must be good. It is this setting up of the devil as evil and God as good which separates us from our opportunity to find physical, mental, moral and financial harmony.

Here is a very simple exercise to follow. Accept in your mind a state of consciousness in which you agree that God is all Power and the only Power; that God is infinite; that God is all-mighty; that beside God there is no other power. In the 43rd chapter of Isaiah we read: "But now thus saith the Lord that created thee, O Jacob, and he that formed thee, O Israel, Fear not: for I have redeemed thee, I have called thee by thy name; thou art mine." If from the time you were a small child you have been taught this one truth, "Fear not: for I have redeemed thee, I have called thee by thy name; thou art mine," would you ever have known fear? "When thou passest through the waters, I will be with thee; and through the rivers, they shall not overflow thee: when thou walkest through the fire, thou shalt not be burned; neither shall the flame kindle upon thee. For I am the Lord thy God, the Holy One of Israel, thy Savior . . . Since thou wast precious in my sight, thou hast been honourable, and I have loved thee." Can you not readily imagine the state of consciousness in which you would live had you been taught exclusively and continually throughout your childhood that God loved you; that God is your God, and He would not permit any evil to befall you? You would be so alive in the consciousness of God as the only Power that you would never fear, nor would you ever lack for any good.

"Yet now hear, O Jacob my servant; and Israel, whom I have chosen: Thus saith the Lord that made thee, and formed thee from the womb, which will help thee; . . . For I will pour water upon him that is thirsty, and floods upon the dry ground: I will pour my spirit upon thy seed, and my blessing upon thine offspring." Throughout our youth we were taught to look only to our parents, but here we learn that God "formed thee from the womb." We were children of God right from the womb, under God's protection, and only God supplied our needs and supported our activities. From everlasting we learn that God alone is the only Power in our lives. In this understanding you can see what would have happened to the devil: never would there have been the fear of evil or the fear of punishment. We would have found a love for God instead of a fear of God, and we would never have believed that God would ever turn His back upon us.

Not only is this Truth being taught in The Infinite Way, but it has been in existence throughout all time and has been known to all peoples. There is only one Power, and God is that Power. There is no power in effect, and there is no power apart from

God. God is the Life and the Being. In the sacred Hindu poem, "Bhagavad-Gita," or "The Song Celestial," translated by Sir Edwin Arnold, we read: "I say to thee weapons reach not the life; flame burns it not, waters cannot o'erwhelm, nor dry winds wither it. Impenetrable, unentered, unassailed, unharmed, untouched, immortal, all-arriving, stable, sure, invisible, ineffable, by word and thought uncompassed, ever all itself, thus is the soul declared?" Here again we see that there is one Life and God is that Life; there is one Power and God is that Power. So it is that with a consciousness filled with the realization of God as the only Power, we cannot fear anything in the realm of effect or in the form of the creature.

Most religious teachings have not given us the truth that God is omnipotent in earth as in heaven, but the day is here when every knee must bend to the truth that there is but one Power. All metaphysical teachings have their origin in the revelation of God as One. But what has happened to that teaching? Mortal mind, which is the modern name for the devil, came along, and so we find the older church people fearing the devil, and the newer ones fearing mortal mind. The wrong and ignorant interpretations of Truth binds us to the belief in two powers, but the answer is always the same: in truth God is the only Power. Everyone of us, to some degree in our human experience, have accepted two powers— a power and presence apart from God; a power that sometimes punishes and sometimes rewards; a power that sometimes cannot reach us—and we are now paying the penalty for such acceptance.

There is no power in effect. There is no power in man-made thought or thing. "For my thoughts are not your thoughts, neither are your ways my ways, saith the Lord. For as the heavens are higher than earth, so are my ways higher than your ways, and my thoughts than your thoughts." However, if we are not spiritually alert, we can be made to accept any kind of false teaching or propaganda if it is thrust upon us frequently and forcefully enough. Through the mass hypnotism of the press and radio we have all been victims of propaganda of one sort or another, but none of that could reach us if we but accepted the teaching that God, the Infinite Invisible, is the only Power.

In our frantic modern day race for supremacy in armaments and material strength it becomes necessary to stop and ask ourselves: Where does all this end? Is superiority and bigness all there is to power? ". . . for by strength shall no man prevail. . . . Be not afraid nor dismayed by reason of this great multitude; for the battle is not yours, but God's. . . . Be strong and courageous, be not afraid nor dismayed for the king of Assyria, nor for all the multitude that is with him: for there be more with us than with him. With him is an arm of flesh; but with us is the Lord our God to help us, and to fight our battles." Those who are materially minded have only the "arm of flesh," but those who recognize God as the only Power can live without fear, and let the external power become as big as it wants. Whether it is a big fever, a big lack, or a big bomb, it is only the "arm of flesh," but we have that which is Invisible. We have that which cannot be touched, for "No weapon that is formed against thee shall prosper. . . ." Just as David went forth to meet Goliath, armed only in faith in God, so can we meet any suggestion of inharmony by our recognition of the one Power.

Out of the teachings of two powers come the philosophies that cause men to disagree among themselves. There is no answer to their questions because they are working with an erroneous premise —good and evil. Always good and evil are wrestling with each other, and what a struggle there is until you can get close to that power of good and get it to help you. But watch what happens when you relinquish the belief in two powers and rest in the consciousness of the Christ. Then it is that you can understand the Master when He said, "Thou couldst have no power at all against me, except it were given thee from above." The Master proved His ministry by saying, "Go and shew John again those things which ye do hear and see: The blind receive their sight, and the lame walk, the lepers are cleansed, and the deaf hear, the dead are raised up, and the poor have the gospel preached to them." The Master submitted to the crucifixion in order to prove there is no power even in death. And He also taught, ". . . all they that take the sword shall perish with the sword."

The mystics of the world, whether Krishna of India, Lao Tze of China, Jesus of Nazareth, or John of Patmos, all have given us the revelation that God is One. The Hebrew mystics knew this truth when they taught, "Hear, O Israel, the Lord our God is one Lord." Throughout scripture you will find, over and over again, the assurances of God's love for His Children: "Fear not: for I have redeemed thee, I have called thee by thy name; thou art mine. . . . Even every one that is called by my name: for I have formed him; yea, I have made him. . . . Ye are my witnesses, saith the Lord and my servant whom I have chosen: that ye may know and believe me, and understand that I am he: before me there was no God formed, neither shall there be after me. I, even I, am the Lord; and beside me there is no savior. . . . I am the first, and I am the last; and beside me there is no God . . . and who, as I, shall call, and shall declare it, and set it in order for me, since I appointed the ancient people? and the things that are coming, and shall come, let them shew unto them. Fear ye not, neither be afraid: have not I told thee from that time, and have declared it? ye are even my witnesses. Is there a God beside me? yea, there is no God; I know not any." And so, again and again, it is revealed that God is one God; that God is one Power.

"They that make a graven image are all of them vanity; and their delectable things shall not profit. . . . Who hath formed a God, or molten a graven image that is profitable for nothing?" Each of us has made an image of God: one looks at it and sees Buddha, another sees Jesus. Each has formed a concept of what he thinks God is, and then begins to worship and pray to that concept. And all the time God is saying, "Only I am God, not your concept. Only I, the Invisible, am God—that alone is God." And so it is that we must stop making images in our minds, stop picturing what God must be like, and trust the unformed Invisible that penetrates and interpenetrates all being.

Understand that "the kingdom of God is within you." Understand that "the place where thou standest is holy ground," and even if it seems, at the moment, to be in hell or in the valley of the shadow of death, God is right there with you. We must cease this nonsensical belief in two powers, this clinging to a belief in a God that punishes and rewards, a God that is present when we experience a healing, and absent when we do not experience the healing we expect. God is never absent from us except in our convictions and fears that there are two powers, and our convictions and fears of other powers which we have set up in our own minds. We not only fear them—we sometimes fear God!

Teaching Truth to Young Children

Truth must be embodied in living, and the only way a child can be taught Truth is in that same embodiment of living. It is for this reason that children must be taught by their parents. The child reflects the atmosphere of its home and its parents, and he naturally absorbs whatever is in the consciousness of his parents. If the mother, especially, has a consciousness of the truth of the Allness of God, whether or not she specifically sets about to teach the child, in the natural course of events the conversation and the general atmosphere will do the teaching.

Many of the methods used to discipline children defeat the purpose of spiritual teaching. Spiritual teaching is not teaching at all: it is a mode of life;

a code of conduct; a matter of consciousness. If the parent has a consciousness of God as the only Power, he cannot impart to the child a fear of any person, place or thing. If a parent really believes that God is the only Law, and places the power of Life in God rather than in food or exercise or human discipline, in what is good or is not good, this realization and awareness of God's Allness and God's Government of Its Creation will be embodied in the child.

For instance, if a parent has the 23rd Psalm in his heart, and really believes that "The Lord is my shepherd: I shall not want. He maketh me to lie down in green pastures; he leadeth me beside the still waters," he will actually impart his own inner confidence and conviction to the child and, therefore, would never convey fear of any kind. The child would *know* that no matter where he went or what he did, whether at school or anywhere else, he would not want for love, understanding, inspiration or any good. Never would he know a fear of playing in the street, a fear of going to school, a fear of contagion or kidnapping.

An hour of Sunday School each week is helpful, practical and useful, but it is not going to change the life of a child. If the Sunday School teacher really knows the truth, he can be a great blessing in that one hour if the parents consistently follow up the teaching at home. Often a child appears to drift away from Sunday School after a few years, and that is either because he has been incorrectly taught or because the rest of the time at home with the parents has offset the teaching. It is impossible and inconsistent to teach a child that all good comes from God, and then turn around and say, "No, you cannot have this or that because you have not been good." It is illogical to teach a child that God is the only Life and the only Power, and then say, "You *must* eat spinach because it is good for you."

Whether the child is two months of age or two years, the consciousness of the parents is reflected in the life-experience of the child. So the responsibility, whether in treatment or in raising the child, is the same. The consciousness of the individual determines what is taking place in his life. Watch the miracles that take place in small children in the wisdom that God is the very center of their being. Watch the changes that occur in behavior and conduct the moment the restrictions of "Thou shalt not" are removed. I have seen it happen that as soon as small children were taught to meditate and realize that the kingdom of God is within their own beings, they quickly began to feel the impulse of God within. Then they learned to turn to the Father within, and consistently they were led, guided and directed. The moment a child realizes that *the Father is within his own being* there is no longer the capacity for disobedience, poor conduct or disrespect.

Once the child becomes aware that he can commune with God, and that he can become silent and let God impart to him, the innocent child-mind quickly touches the Presence of God within his own being. With the removal of the human whip of "Thou shalt not," you will find him God-directed and God-governed.

We, as adults, are just a wee bit slower than the children, but we get there, too.

The Infinite Way in the Home

A family unit can be likened to any unit which works together as one body to bring out a finished result. It can be compared to an orchestra, wherein each member constantly practices on his particular instrument in order to bring out the inherent perfection within. Over all, guiding and synchronizing the whole, is the conductor, changing here, suggesting there, always with the knowledge uppermost that his is the role of bringing out the perfection of each instrument; patiently standing by, aiding in drawing out the best in each member. Never is one member of the orchestra able to take the place of another, except as a temporary measure. Always each has his own complete and distinct function.

In the working out of The Infinite Way principles in our daily living, we can see how each member of a family unit is alone responsible for his God-contact, his God-awareness. As mothers of small children we are very much aware of our role of conductor— sometimes feeling it more in the nature of a policeman—but if uppermost in the mother's mind is the understanding of her true identity, and the identity of the little ones with whom she is dealing, her function becomes simpler and lovelier.

Each time of communion with the members of her family brings its own reward. This does not necessarily mean the old idea of family prayer or a time especially set aside. Many deep and wonderful things hidden in the heart of a child are revealed in such every-day experiences as meal-time, bed-time, bath-hour, and that very important "snuggle-time" with the tiniest ones. Truly precious are some of the thoughts that are exchanged, and a mother knows, too, that in such times she has learned more of God.

Just as it is vitally important to keep an openness to God, so it is with family relationships. It is equally important to develop and maintain a feeling of reciprocity and co-operation with each member of the family. There cannot be a wall or a sense of separation existing between any members, young or old, without all being aware of it. Even if nothing has been said, it seeps through the household like a damp fog, like the mist that it is, chilling all members. There is an inner communication needed in family relationships which must be left open at all times. You will know when you have this contact, because when the channel is clear, the way is clear. Viewpoints may differ, procedures may vary, but always the end result is harmony—Love in action.

In their sense of duty to their families, mothers develop a habit of formulating a course of action—a goal. This is alright as far as it goes, but it cannot stop there. As a child is taught to turn within for its guidance, one will quickly see the harmonious unfolding of its life's work. Truly, life lived in this fashion is what the Master meant when He said, "For my yoke is easy, and my burden is light."

(A Student.)

Across the Desk

Frequently the questions are asked: Why is it that sometimes my prayer or treatment is instantly effective and harmony restored, even in seemingly serious difficulties—whereas, at other times, there is little or no noticeable improvement? Why are there some days when all my affairs proceed smoothly when harmony is a continuous experience, and peace and quiet reign—and then, for a while it is as if God had entirely forgotten and forsaken me?

The answer is that on those good days, when the quick and beautiful healings occur, and when life is a constant flow of harmonious experiences, you have found your inner one-ness or *realization of God*. On the other days, no doubt you have meditated as usual, gone through the routine of knowing the Truth, acknowledged God as the central theme of all existence, and declared the One Power, the One Infinite Presence—and yet have not made the inner contact which reveals Emmanuel or "God with us."

The Infinite Way is constituted of two parts: the metaphysical, which is the letter of Truth; the mystical, which is conscious union with God, the actual realization and attainment of the Presence of God. Students often forget that the letter of Truth and the knowing of Truth are but steps leading up to the actual realization of God, or attainment of ". . . this mind . . . which was also in Christ Jesus."

Until one is far along on the spiritual Path, it may be necessary to consciously meditate on some scriptural or metaphysical quotation, and to recall and declare as much Truth as possible. It may be wise to bring to conscious remembrance much Truth about God, Christ, and individual being; and to remember that there is but One Power, One Presence, One Law, Substance, Cause and Being. This is for one purpose: to lift oneself into the atmosphere of

God where the Spirit takes over and becomes the law, substance, activity and life of oneself, one's affairs, and those of one's world of patients, students, family or business.

Having achieved the conscious "feeling" of the Presence, the assurance of well-being, or the "click" that announces God-in-action, you have attained an atmosphere of the Christ that "performeth the thing that is appointed for me," which "will perfect that which concerneth me." Then it is that the healing-work, teaching, or other activity of your day will be successful, joyous, peaceful and prosperous. Failure to attain this conscious experience of God will leave you with only your human strength and wisdom with which to meet the strife and struggles of the world.

Students of The Infinite Way should never expect much of that day in which God's Presence is not realized. Do we not know, only too well, that "I can of mine own self do nothing"? Have we not learned, through bitter experience, that without the actual attainment of Christ we are nothing, and can do nothing of any spiritual nature? Have we not experienced the supreme joy of spiritual living when, like Paul, we could say, "I can do all things through Christ which strengtheneth me"? O Students!—believe me—it were better to arise at three o'clock in the morning and remain in meditation and study until that overshadowing of the Spirit takes place, than to sleep the hours away and be compelled to face the day without the glorious feeling of being in the Spirit!

The healing and teaching work is not difficult—

truly the ministry is a joy beyond words when the student is centered in God, and walks through the day with the spiritual impulse tingling in mind and body. When one has been touched by the Christ, one's patient or student will be stirred and drawn into God's Presence and restored. However, do not expect much of the prayer, meditation or treatment that is not given right from the Soul or Spirit.

In His Presence is fulness of life; resurrection and ascension. In Him is peace, joy and dominion. In His Spirit is rest, relaxation, restoration and renewal. "Thou wilt shew me the path of life: in thy presence is fulness of joy; at thy right hand there are pleasures for evermore."

Wisdoms of the Infinite Way

"Prayer is the absence of desire in the recognition of *Is*.

"Prayer is an awareness of that which *Is*, by 'seeing' it—not making it so.

"Prayer is the inner Vision of harmony. This Vision is attained by giving up the desire to change or improve any one or any thing.

"To pray is to *become aware* of the harmony which *Is*, without a mental effort on your part.

"Never seek any thing or any condition in prayer. *Let* harmony define and *reveal itself*. Let your prayer be *letting the Is appear*."

CHAPTER SIX

HIGHER VIEWS OF GOD, PRAYER AND THE SELF

VERY little progress can be made on the spiritual Path of life until we have caught some vision of what God is, and what God's function is in our experience. This subject must be approached in a very relaxed manner and with very relaxed thought. We are going to ask ourselves questions about God which will lead us to the subject of prayer. We want to take nothing for granted, and so we ask: What is the place and function of God in my life? What kind of a God have I? What do I want and expect from God? What can God do for me?

The normal concept is that of a God, apart from us or within us, who has all our good but is withholding it. Usually, in going to God, we are seeking to get something from God—health, supply, opportunity, companionship—something which we believe is being withheld. Yes, it seems that God has all these things, but is not granting them, so we pray for them. And sometimes, if our prayers are not granted quickly enough, we make all sorts of promises which, often, we have no intention of keeping.

Even now, in our more enlightened state of consciousness, that is the attitude of many. We have in mind a God who *can* bestow good, but who is not *doing* it. We often censure ourselves, and believe that some evil act of omission or commission is the reason God is withholding from us. Many physicians will tell you that many of the ills of the world are caused by guilt-complexes, wherein people are holding themselves in condemnation: sometimes for some serious offence committed in the past, but more often for small and inconsequential acts. Even if God had a good memory (which He has not) He probably would have forgotten by now. God has no memory of our faults and failings, and never, in the history of the world, has God punished a sinner. The sinner is punished by his own act of sin, not by any act of God. There are certain Laws of God, and if we violate these laws we pay the penalty. God does not know that the law has been violated, so never hold in thought that God is withholding your good because of sin. If you believe that you are being punished by God, your concept of God is entirely erroneous.

God is not a withholding God, neither is He a giving God. God never gives nor bestows anything! God is Love, and because God is Love, God is forever loving. There is no love in withholding and no love in punishment. God is Love. God is *being* Love. God is Life. God is *being* Life. God is not withholding life, nor is God going to bestow life, since God, Itself, *is* Life, and there is no unexpressed Life, in the same way that the sun is not withholding sunshine, it has no sunshine to give. *The sun is shining!* There is no use praying to God—*God is being!* If God were withholding something you needed, or if God were waiting for you to be good or deserving, or to find the right form of prayer or method of treatment, He would be a cruel and severe God indeed. God has nothing to give, and God will never give more than He is giving you now!

God *Is*, Life *Is*, Love *Is*—know this truth and this truth will set you free from the belief that you must go to God for anything. We pay lip-service to the fact that God is the All-knowing Mind, but too often we say, "I need this, and I want that." Far from accepting the Christian doctrine of an All-knowing and All-loving God, we persist in telling Him that we lack rent money, food, clothing, employment, companionship, health. We profess to be followers of Christ-teaching, but are we not contradicting ourselves when we say, "God is the All-knowing Mind," and then go ahead and pray for things and conditions? The Master tells us it is not necessary to pray for food, clothing, or anything else, because, "Your Father knoweth that ye have need of these things," . . . and . . . " it is your Father's good pleasure to give you the kingdom."

James says: "Ye ask, and receive not, because ye ask amiss. . . ." Every time we go to God for something, and every time we expect something from God, we pray amiss. There is only one way to pray, and it is so very simple: "Thank you, Father. Thank you." God *is* the All-knowing Mind, the Infinite Intelligence of this universe. No one has to tell God to make grass green or roses red; no one has to tell God when the stars shall come out, or when the tides shall change. Shall we, then, tell God that we are in need of anything? We have been praying amiss for thousands of years.

In recent years we have come to enlightened, spiritual, metaphysical, scientific Christianity, and now we twist our prayers around into affirmations and denials, but for the very same purpose that formerly we used petition. Now, instead of praying, "Oh God! Heal my child," we say, "My child is perfect," and then wait to see if God makes him so. We are living in an age enlightened in everything of a material and mental nature. Let this also be a spiritually enlightened age. Let us acknowledge openly that our God is the Infinite Intelligence of the universe; that our God is Divine Love. When we have that kind of a God, our prayer is never a seeking or asking, never a beseeching or affirming: our prayer is a continuous, "Thank you, Father."

Let us see where we are at this minute with our concept of God and our ideas of prayer. Let us see if we are having an expanding, broader, more comprehensive idea of God. Can we now see, since God is Infinite, Divine, Spiritual Love, that there is no need for our asking God to be love, or to give love? Is it not clear that if ours is a God that knows how to produce a pearl in an oyster, petroleum in the earth, a God that directs the birds in their flight, is not this Infinite Intelligence sufficient to be the governing and guiding influence in our experience without our offering any information or suggestions?

The function of God is really that of an eternal Life, which, at the same time, is an Infinite Intelligence and a Divine Love, operating within Itself. "I and my Father are one . . . and he that seeth me seeth him that sent me." God the Father, God the Son—functioning within Itself, right where you are.

As you relax in that realization, It takes over and It functions harmoniously, joyously, abundantly. But the very moment you turn to It with any sense of getting, informing, desiring or even hoping, *you prevent its operation in your experience.* You are placing your finite concepts and views between you and the Infinite. You interfere with the flow of God the moment you go to God with a desire, a fear, a doubt, a concern, or even a hope. You go to God with clean hands and a pure heart only when you can say, with conviction and trust, "Thy Will be done in earth, as it is in heaven," and then *refuse* to entertain any concept of what God's Will should be. You stand in the Divine Presence, pure of heart, when you have no finite will, no personal desires, hopes or ambitions, but in the utter and complete realization: "I am thine, Thou art mine. I am in Thee, and Thou art in me. Thy Will be done in me."

How often we say that and then, in some way, outline what our hopes or desires or ambitions may be. We seem to think that if those hopes or desires are good that makes it alright—we only desire our children to be healthy and well-behaved, and our neighbor to be successful. If God is the All-knowing Mind, the Infinite Intelligence and Wisdom of the universe, the Divine Love and the only Power, why desire at all? Why not let God's Wisdom reveal Itself? Why not let God's Love unfold and disclose Itself within you? If you pray and do not receive an answer, it is because you are praying amiss. In some way you are pretending a greater wisdom than that of God, and you may even be pretending a greater love than that of God. If desire is for things or conditions, it is sin.

True prayer is an absolute conviction that God is intelligence and love; that there is no power apart from God, no power in opposition or conflict with God. Therefore, *nothing* is interfering with God's love for His Children. Nothing that you can do will influence God to be more than God nor less than God. Watch what happens as you begin to accept this kind of a God, and no longer reach out, but merely stand still in being and say, *"God is."* What greater prayer than those two words? *God is*, and as long as *God is*, why should you be concerned? Your only concern should be if you still doubt that *God is*. On the whole, much of the world doubts God or they would not waste so much time praying for this or that. If they really believed that God is Divine Intelligence and Love, why would they spend all this time trying to influence God? *God is*—Thy Grace *is* my sufficiency in all things, is the acknowledgment of the Presence, the Wisdom, the Love and the Power of God in your experience.

We shall go back now to a previous statement: There is no withholding God, and there is no giving God. God is a state of eternal and immortal *being*; a state of Infinite Intelligence and Divine Love. The Life of God cannot be lengthened nor can it be shortened. The Life of God cannot age nor can it change. God is a state of eternal, immortal, infinite Being of Good. ". . . God is light, and in him is no darkness at all . . . and God is able to make all grace abound toward you; that ye, always having all sufficiency in all things, may abound to every good work." That should be our attitude of prayer.

The acknowledgment of Divine Grace is prayer. In the light of the recognition of God as that which needs no enlightenment as to what we need, desire, or think we should have, prayer, then, is a recognition of the nature of God. Prayer also is a recognition of our relationship to God. Our relationship to God is Oneness, but sometimes our prayers would make it appear that we were poor, insignificant little creatures, praying up to a great Deific Being who holds our fate in His hands. That passes for humility, in spite of the fact that scripture says, "Son, thou art ever with me, and all that I have is thine." We are not less than God: we are co-existent with God. We are the Children of God, "And if children, then heirs: heirs of God, and joint-heirs with Christ." How, then, could the Son pray a prayer of petition, seeking or asking of the Father? Your heavenly Father knoweth your needs, but if you outline what that need is, you are putting forth your own concepts in such a way as to believe that you can inform or influence God to bring it about. Our Divine Father need not be reminded of His duty to us. All we must do is acknowledge God, acknowledge the all-knowingness of the All-knowing Mind, the all-lovingness of Divine Love; acknowledge the All-power of That which knows no other power than Its own infinite nature and being.

The heading over the 23rd Psalm reads: "David's confidence in God's Grace." "The Lord *is* my shepherd; I shall not want." That one line is enough of a prayer. As you continue reading this beautiful poem, you become aware of the continuous assurance of God's love, and you will notice that it does not contain one word of appeal to God.

As you approach something of this concept of God and prayer (which is vastly different from the world's concept) you will come to understand another reason for failure in prayer. As a rule, and even in metaphysics, we pray to God in the expectancy or hope of something that is to emanate *from* God, or *through* God. We set up a sort of triangle in which we, down here, pray to God, up there, for something, out there. In other words, God is a way-station, a means through which we hope to achieve something. But the truth is, that God and I and whatever I am praying for are *one*—"I and my Father are one . . . all things that the Father hath are mine"—*it is already established!*

God is the substance of all form, God is infinite, God is all-inclusive, so the only thing to pray for is the realization of God. *God* is my life, my supply, my high tower, my fortress, but let us not ask for a translation of that in human terms. Just let it be spiritual, and you will find that ". . . your life is hid with Christ in God." But, because God is infinite, when you make your contact with God you find supply, companionship, housing, health, wholeness, immortality and eternality *included in God.* It is when you think of God as the *means* toward that which you desire that your hopes will be dashed to earth. If your prayer does not *stop at God*, there is no answer.

Prayer is recognition, prayer is abiding in confidence, and we align ourselves with all of the Good of God through this prayer of acknowledgment—

Thy Grace is my sufficiency in *all* things—and then rest and let that sufficiency appear in accord with God's Will. If He wants to make that appear as a home, a marriage, a business—fine, let us follow where He leads. But let us never attempt to *direct* God! Let us make a greater effort to watch ourselves each time we are tempted to pray for something. Instead, let our prayer be that we may have the recognition of God Itself, and we will find that that will suffice.

Let us have no hopes, no desires, no expectations beyond that of realizing the Omnipresence of God. Therein can desire be prayer. Desire *is* prayer, if the desire is for God alone, but the moment desire goes beyond that, it is sin. *God is all*, therefore pray for *God*. God already is your being, therefore let your prayer be this calm assurance of God's Grace, the complete confidence in God's Presence, Wisdom and Love. "Thy Grace, Thy Love, Thy Wisdom is my sufficiency in all things," is the greatest prayer that can be uttered, and if you never know another that will be enough.

Rising to Grace

There are three major points of the Message of The Infinite Way which must be thoroughly embodied within the consciousness of each student. The first is the nature of God. Each student must change his concepts of God, of his relationship to God, of the function of God in his experience. The second is the nature of prayer. Each must learn the nature of prayer. No prayer that has ever been spoken, read, or heard is sufficient, and so he must attain a much higher concept of prayer. The only true prayer is recognition, acknowledgment and confidence in the Omnipresence of God. The only way to pray is through communion with God, without a single desire, and with no attempt to enlighten, persuade or influence God. The third point is the nature of error. When you know the nature of God and your relationship to God, and when you know the nature of prayer, you can then see error or evil only as a mirage, an illusion, a nothingness which has been frightening you with an appearance.

When you come to an understanding of these things, you come to the highest point of The Infinite Way Message in which you realize that *because God is what God is* God's All-ness makes nothing else necessary. Since God is Omnipresent, harmony is omnipresent, supply is omnipresent, love is omnipresent—now what do you want God to do for you? Since error has been seen as a mirage, what need have you for God's power? Then it is that you become aware of the fact that it is not up to God— it is up to *you*! It is up to you to bring yourself into alignment with That which *already is*!

God is, eternally—God has been from the beginning, God changeth never, God is with you until the end of the world. You need to lift *your* concept of God, of your own identity, of prayer, and of the impotence of evil. When you have done that you are living and moving and having your being in God. Can you imagine going to heaven and still being in need of God? Why, no! You would be basking in God's Presence and His Love. You can go to heaven right here and now by giving up all beliefs that you must reach out to God for anything, or do other than *let God take over.*

The responsibility is upon you to attain a higher concept of God, a higher respect for God, a greater love for God, and a greater trust in the infinite nature of God's All-ness, Wisdom and Love. You must also have a greater respect for your own identity, a greater realization of what it means to be the Son of the most High, of what it means to live in God-consciousness, under God's supervision, government and direction. You must learn to relax and rest in the realization that *God is.* As long as there is a God, *I am.* As long as God *is,* an Infinite Intelligence is operating. As long as God *is,* a Divine Love is functioning. As long as God *is,* there is no other power. As long as God *is,* that is your assurance and acknowledgment of Him in all your ways. And with that understanding your prayer is one of gratitude: "Thank you, Father, Thy Grace *is* my sufficiency in all things, and I seek nothing more. In Thee I live and move and have my being. In Thee I find my hiding place from the world's beliefs that there is a power of sin, a power of disease, a power of lack. I seek no more, I search no more— in this calm, confident assurance of Thy Grace, I rest. I am in Thee, and Thou art in me, and we are One." And so it is that you must not acquaint God with what you think you need, nor enlighten God as to what you would like. You must have but one pure desire—". . . that they (you) might know thee the only true God . . ." whom to know aright is life eternal.

"And Jesus answered him, The first of all the

commandments is, Hear, O Israel; the Lord our God is one Lord: And thou shalt love the Lord thy God with all thy heart, and with all thy soul, and with all thy mind, and with all thy strength: this is the first commandment. And the second is like, namely this, Thou shalt love thy neighbor as thyself. There is none other commandment greater than these." This teaching of the Master is the basis of the Message of The Infinite Way, and any truth about the Master is the truth about you and about me, in proportion to *our* conscious awareness of it.

Another major principle is this: "For unto everyone that hath shall be given, and he shall have abundance: but from him that hath not shall be taken away even that which he hath." To those who acknowledge, "I have Thy Grace, and that is my sufficiency," shall be given, but to those who deny that they have, and who are eternally seeking, from them shall be taken even that which they have.

In the beautiful words of the Psalmist, we read: "Give unto the Lord the glory due unto his name; worship the Lord in the beauty of holiness." And so we come to another principle: "Thou shalt not bear false witness against thy neighbor." It makes no difference if your neighbor is black, white or yellow, Hebrew, Christian or pagan—your neighbor is the self-same being: *God expressed, God manifest in flesh.* This is the beauty of holiness. This is knowing the truth about your neighbor; this is praying for your neighbor; this is forgiving your neighbor, even as you would have your neighbor forgive you. "Love worketh no ill to his neighbor: therefore love is the fulfilling of the law."

Our Message is one of Love, and we are fulfilling the law of Love in our acknowledgment of the infinite nature of God, and the eternal nature of the Son of God. In our acknowledgment of Omnipresence, Omnipotence, Omniscience, we have acknowledged Divine Grace. We have acknowledged that the Grace of God is for us, for our neighbor, and for our enemy. In this acknowledgment we seek forgiveness of our errors of ignorance, and just as freely we forgive all others in this realization that this truth is the truth about everyone in heaven, on earth, or in hell. "Thou shalt love thy neighbor as thyself . . . forgive and ye shall be forgiven . . .", and in this instant of realization we release all those who are holding themselves in bondage to false concepts of God, Law, Love and Life. We loose them and let them go, in the realization that all that is of God is Good—and what is there that is not of God?

Oh! What a wonderful thing it is to know that *there is nothing to go to God for*!

Conscious Union with God

In order to enter into the mystical life one must master the ability to remain in the silence without thought, and this is the most difficult part of all spiritual living. In no way is this a cessation or repression of thought, nor an effort toward such: instead, it is attaining such deep communion with God that thought stops of its own accord. The first step toward this is that of having nothing to pray for, because it is in the moment that you come to the place where you acknowledge that there is nothing to pray for that you have God. Then it is that God is your Soul, your Being, your Father. Then it is that "I and my Father are one," and I am heir to all the heavenly riches. In that moment of realization you are enabled to understand that the Divine Mind, or Cosmic Consciousness, is an Infinite Intelligence imbued with love, and It functions as your being when conscious thinking has been stilled.

In your everyday walk of life, you may have one plan in mind and the Cosmic Mind may have another, but this you will never know as long as you are busily engaged in thinking, planning, routing, scheming, listening and reacting to all the activities and distractions of the external world. In order to receive the Divine Grace of the Cosmic Mind or Intelligence, there must be periods of complete quiet for the thinking mind. This does not mean that your mind must or will become a total blank, but it does mean that throughout the day and night you must have several periods in which you desire nothing more than the joy of inner communion with God. It is in this complete stillness and relaxation from thought that the Father takes over in your experience.

Our Master spent much time in silent meditation and communion, and you can be assured that He was not talking or asking God for anything. He was listening. He was listening for God's direction and instruction, guidance and support, and then He was enabled to say: "Believest thou not that I am in the Father, and the Father in me? The words that I speak unto you I speak not of myself: but the Father that dwelleth in me, he doeth the works." And so it is that before one can enter into the mystical or Cosmic Life, one must transform from the habit of continuously thinking to that of continuously listening.

The Cosmic Life does not always mean the spiritual or religious life. For instance, every composer, poet and writer, every designer and inventor, every architect and builder of any note, has touched the Cosmic. They are taught by something within their own being, but that could not occur if they did not possess an innate ability to be silent and listen. It may open the world of music, literature, art, science or business, but it will come as a result of the faculty to be still, to listen, to hear and to receive Cosmic or universal impulses. Those who are attuned to the Cosmic Mind without the religious influence are they who have brought forth the great works on the human plane.

When the Cosmic touches the religious life it is called the mystical life. The dictionary defines "mysticism" as the doctrine or belief that direct knowledge of God, of spiritual truth, etc., is attainable through immediate intuition or insight and in a way differing from ordinary sense perception or the use of logical reasoning; any type of theory asserting the possibility of attaining knowledge or power through faith or spiritual insight. In other words, mysticism is a teaching or religion which believes in conscious union with God; with the ability to achieve direct contact with God and to receive answers to prayer. A mystic is an individual who has touched God at some time or another, or one who is in constant communion with God, and who receives all of his impulses from God. A mystic usually is attuned to the religious, ethical and moral life, and often shows it forth in poetry or writing or painting as did Emerson, Whitman, Blake and the many known religious mystics.

We can understand and live the mystical life of conscious communion with God only when we change from the conscious thinking mind to the universal Mind which is ever ready to pour Itself through us. In order to make this change we must become quiet and still, and let the human mind become the instrument through which the Cosmic or God Mind expresses itself.

No matter how gifted an artist or writer or scientist may be, he still needs technical training. The Spirit flows, but the human mind brings it down into practical and workable experience. That is why, in the other realm, there must be practice, practice and more practice. So, also, it is with us: the listening mind must become attuned to God. God reveals Itself to us, but we must constantly practice until that time comes when the Spirit so completely takes over that nothing is necessary in the way of conscious mental work.

There is a Mind, or Soul Consciousness, which is God, and we become consciously aware of It only in the degree of our listening ability and our receptivity. It is in developing that listening ability and receptivity that the mind quiets and becomes stilled to such a degree that it becomes an avenue or instrument through which that which we call God manifests and expresses Itself.

Study, read, ponder, think and meditate, but also have frequent moments of listening so that the fullness of It can come to you. No truth that you read or know in your own mind is a spiritual power. The spiritual power is the Spirit, imparting Itself to you when you are silently listening, hearing and feeling. Always remember that it is not the truth you speak or write or know that heals: it is the Word of God, of which you become aware within your own being, that rolls back the Red Sea, brings manna from the sky, heals the sick and raises the dead. It is not your knowledge, your wisdom nor your understanding—it is God's, and you become the instrument through which God works.

The Eternal *You*

The harmony of your existence depends upon your understanding of the subject of immortality, and the correct understanding of immortality lies in knowing that *you* are the Life and Law of your body and being.

If you will turn to the illustration of the orange tree, as given in the chapter "Supply" in *The Infinite Way*,[1] you will learn that the invisible spiritual law, operating in and as the tree, is the crop; and that the actual oranges on the tree represent the fruitage or the result of the crop. Even after the oranges have been sold or otherwise disposed of, the crop has not been touched: the crop remains in the life of the tree, to appear and re-appear. The trunk of the tree is not the tree: that also is but an effect. The seed is not the tree until the life-force causes the activity which results in sprouting, rooting, and progressing up to the visible tree and fruitage. The

[1] By Joel S. Goldsmith.

law of Life, acting upon the seed, does the work. The real tree is the *life* of the tree. There is an invisible law of Life acting upon everything in the universe, and it is this life-force, which we call Spirit, or God, that is the real substance, law and activity of one's being.

You are Consciousness, and regardless of what happens to the physical body, *you* remain. God constitutes your being. Life-force constitutes your being. Soul constitutes your being. *You* are Life, Mind, Soul, and you are immortal and eternal. The tree cannot bear fruit except as it is constituted and permeated by the life-force, and as you begin to comprehend your true identity you will see that your body can never know the fruitage of health, harmony and continuity unless you realize that "The Lord thy God in the midst of thee is mighty."

The Master taught that, "Before Abraham was, I am ... I will never leave thee, nor forsake thee ... I am with you alway, even unto the end of the world. . . . Destroy this temple, and in three days I will raise it up." We have made the mistake of believing that the Master meant that Jesus would never leave you nor forsake you, that Jesus would be with you until the end of the world, that Jesus would build the temple again. This is not the Master's meaning at all: He taught that "I am the way, the truth, and the life. . . . For the bread of God is he which cometh down from heaven, and giveth life unto the world." Once you begin to understand that "I" is the invisible Life, Intelligence and Soul of your being, you will understand why you are immortal. Then you will be able to make your transition as did Moses, Enoch, Elijah and the Master, because you will realize that *you* will never die. You will never know death as long as you do not confuse yourself with the visible tree, or the crop of the tree, but realize yourself to be the life-force Itself.

In living the Infinite Way we are not demonstrating persons or things: we are demonstrating God or Consciousness. We are demonstrating the realization of our God-being, and so we can see that right identification of ourselves is necessary to our spiritual demonstration. "I am come that they might have life, and that they might have it more abundantly." The life-force which you are, and which constitutes your only real and true being, has come that your whole experience may be joyous, peaceful, harmonious, whole, complete, perfect, eternal and immortal.

Another Name

"Aloneness" has been granted me.
Whether on Bishop Street at noon,
Or Kalakaua;
On Waikiki at sunset,
On the sands at Kailua,
Before dawn,
I am alone.
I walk alone in crowds
And feel the solitary Self
In the moonlight on the beach.

"Aloneness" has been granted me.
To walk with men,

To fly the skies,
And sail the seas,
Wherever heart is raised to Him—
I walk alone.
At heat of day,
Or cool of eve,
On shore or city street,
The yearning Soul receives my Aloneness.

The sick are healed.
The restless are forgiven.
Alone, yet in the hearts
Of those who long for peace.
The restless feel my Aloneness;
The hungry eat it;
The thirsty drink it;
It washes the impure minds
Of those who do not know,
Touching the mind with Light.

"Aloneness" has been granted me.
Alone I sit behind the prison wall;
I pace the sickroom floor;
Wherever danger threatens,
My aloneness breaks the spell.
Where misery loves company,
My aloneness they may share.

Alone, I wake, and walk, and sleep—
Alone, I sit or stand.
Alone, I travel sea and sky
And sometimes till the land.
Alone, I walk and talk with men

Or stroll the shady lane.
"Aloneness" has been granted me
Wherever you may be

Across the Desk

During the Spring of 1955, many students have visited Hawaii for instruction and meditation, and I find the words of a meditation are being fulfilled: "Your home is the House of God, wherein He dwells; it is a refuge for those seeking rest; a haven of security; a temple of devotion to His Children. Your home shelters those who seek Him, while on the journey."

To enter the consciousness where God lives one's life, is to meet others who have received the Grace of realizing the Christ life. This communion is a joyous as well as a holy experience. Most of the days and all of the nights I am alone, except for these periods of spiritual refreshment with students and friends of the Way of God.

We are all invited to this feast, and the price is merely giving up concern for one's own welfare. This ability also comes by Grace, but the preparation for receiving Grace is our responsibility. Our periods of study, meditation, reading and hearing the Word; our devotion to the principle of "My *Grace* is sufficient for thee"; our seeking God for God-experience—herein is our preparation for Grace.

"And he spake many things unto them in parables, saying, Behold, a sower went forth to sow: and when he sowed, some seeds fell by the way side, and the fowls came and devoured them up: Some fell upon stony places, where they had not much

earth: and forthwith they sprung up, because they
had no deepness of earth: and when the sun was
up, they were scorched; and because they had no
root, they withered away. And some fell among
thorns; and the thorns sprung up, and choked them:
But other fell into good ground, and brought forth
fruit, some an hundredfold, some sixtyfold, some
thirtyfold. Who hath ears to hear, let him hear."
The seed—the Word—can only become fruit as we
prepare the soil.

The windows in our homes are of no value, in or
of themselves, except as instruments through which
light and air can enter. We are God's windows,
through which His Light and atmosphere of wholeness can penetrate to human consciousness, and
dispel it. Our periods of meditation (when no thought
of self enters) enable us to be windows through which
God enters the human scene, and transmutes it into
Heaven on earth. This we must remember, we are
nothing of ourselves. Do not speak, or write or teach
until His voice utters or His pen writes. There is no
power, no Truth, in what you or I have to give, but
only in That which flows through us. When nothing
comes, be still.

*　　　*　　　*

Certain basic truths must be held in thought until
they become a part of your consciousness. As consciousness becomes imbued with these truths, they
rebuild the fabric of your lives, morally, physically,
mentally and financially.

"Prayer is the Word of God which comes to

you when you are silent enough, still enough, expectant to receive it."
(*Spiritual Interpretation of Scripture*, p. 174.)[1]

"My conscious oneness with God constitutes my oneness with every spiritual idea. That spiritual idea will express itself as a home, a friend . . . book or teacher . . . anything of which I have need."
(*Metaphysical Notes*, p. 39.)[1]

"The cause of the world's trouble is the sense of separation from God. The antidote for the world's trouble is the conscious awareness of God as omnipresent, omnipotent, omniscient—the Reality of Being."
(*The Master Speaks*, p. 50.)[1]

"No matter where an individual finds himself, he will have found the secret of practical and spiritual living if he will follow a program of spiritualizing thought, and of steadfastly holding thought to God throughout the day. Let your first thought in the morning be a conscious awareness of the Presence of God. Carry that awareness with you throughout the day and when retiring at night. Live in the conscious awareness of God, and let that unfold and carry you where it will."
(*Truth for Business and Professional People*, pp. 31-2.)[1]

Again let me remind you: if you are still seeking anything on the outer plane to bring you

[1] By Joel S. Goldsmith.

peace, joy, security or freedom—forget it now! The Infinite Invisible is your rock, your meat, wine and water; your fortress and your high tower.

Wisdoms of the Infinite Way

"Be sure that your prayer is not an attempt to influence God.

"Be sure that your prayer is not a desire to improve God's universe.

"Have no desires in the world. Let God's Grace suffice.

"There are no powers of evil external to yourself. 'Why do the heathen rage, and the people imagine a vain thing?'

"There is an insight in man that visions through all appearances. Be at peace.

"Abide in the deep well of contentment. *I am. It is.*"

CHAPTER SEVEN

MEDITATION FOR BEGINNERS

FEW people disbelieve in God. Most people are convinced that there is a God, or that there is a Divine Power of some sort, but they are not sure just what It is. There was a time when they were content to believe that there was a God in Heaven whom they would meet after death, but in this practical age, particularly, not many are satisfied with that kind of a God. In this present age, the cry is that in spite of all the great mechanical and material advancement in the world, very little progress has been made in the way of spiritual development and unfoldment. Actually, this is not true, because every bit of this mechanical and material development is really the outward expression of inward spiritual power. Our greatest inventors, discoverers and scientists have all been spiritually endowed men; men who have lived close to God, and who have had actual God-contact. Many of the greatest physicists of today are in complete agreement not only that God is a reality, but that God is evident in our human world.

All through the ages there have been spiritually endowed men and women who have had conscious contact with God, who have known conscious union with God, and who have brought this Presence and Power into their actual experience. Always there has been a Lao Tse, a Buddha, a Jesus, a John, a Paul, but none of them ever had wide followings very far beyond their personal circle. None of them were ever widely known, nor their teachings widely practiced—not during their own times or for long periods thereafter.

Every one of these great spiritual leaders is in agreement on these basic principles and teachings: Do unto others as you would have others do unto you; Thou shalt not kill; Thou shalt not steal; Thou shalt not commit adultery; Thou shalt have one God. They did not teach that we all be of the same race, color or creed—they taught the principles of live, let live; love, share, co-operate. If the several hundred million who profess the teachings of Lao Tse, Buddha or Jesus really practiced and lived them, there could never be a war. Later, as the teachings of the great spiritual masters were organized, the religious forms and ceremonies were practiced, but not the original religions. It is for this reason that the world has gone downward, morally and spiritually, to where today nine-tenths of the world is at war, actually or potentially. This represents the degree in which mankind has become separated from the God-power or God-presence which has been revealed through these great mystics as possible to all men.

The questions that are occupying the thoughts of people all over the world today, are: How can we make God available in our experience? How can we bring the God-power to us as, for instance, did Jesus in healing the sick, raising the dead, feeding the poor? How can we make the Presence and Power of God practical in our experience, so as to have a principle with which to work which will enable us to rise above the level of human existence?

We begin to understand how this is accomplished through some of the revelations of these spiritual masters. We are taught by the Master Christian that the kingdom of God, the Presence and Power of God is within you. Jesus called this Presence and Power "Father," and He said, "The Father that dwelleth in me, he doeth the works." Paul, using a different term, said, "I can do all things through Christ which strengtheneth me." It makes no difference what you call this power—God, Father, or the Christ, by whatever name you call It, *It is to be found within you!*

The kingdom of God is within you, not in churches nor in organizations, not in holy mountains nor yet in the temple at Jerusalem, and if we would really believe this great wisdom it would be enough to cause us to leave the world for a season until such time as we could reach, touch and respond to the Father within. Then, when we had made our God-contact, it would be revealed that the whole of the Godhead is to be found within our individual being.

The sure method of making that contact was discovered, many, many centuries ago, through the practice of meditation. The enlightened and educated peoples of India, China, Japan and other Oriental countries learned how to retire into meditation, and there find peace, harmony and joy, even in the midst of world tribulation. In the eighteenth century the Quakers brought meditation into this country, but the Occidental teachings did not accept it, and so it did not spread beyond their own groups.

Meditation is the way to contact the Presence and Power within each individual so as to bring forth this Power of God into expression, into manifestation and into evidence. The question naturally arises: For one who has not learned the art of inner silence, how is meditation accomplished?

The ultimate of meditation is attaining a state of complete silence within. This is not simple of accomplishment because there is no way to stop thought. However, there is a way of meditating which eventually will lead to all thought ceasing of its own accord, leaving one in a sublime state of inner quiet in which come only those thoughts which emanate from God. There are many, many ways of meditating, but, for the beginner in meditation, it is important to avoid trying to accomplish something beyond his immediate understanding. In order to meditate without losing the thread, and without permitting disturbing extraneous thoughts to enter, the mode of contemplative meditation is simple, and will lead one, step by step, into the higher forms of meditation. Even before that it will result in an inner experience that will be one's assurance that the inner contact has been made.

Let us review what we know about the nature of God and the nature of prayer, and then see how our meditations can fit into that. In the Infinite Way Writings, it is revealed that God is a state of divine being, ever-present, ever-available, filling all space. God has nothing to give, and no power to withhold. God is the creative principle and power, the maintaining and sustaining influence of this universe. God is being God all of the time, and He is being

God without direction or petition on our part, and without affirmation or prayer of any nature.

As this is being written there is no sun in the heavens—it is nighttime, yet there is no trace of fear about tomorrow. It would be useless to pray that the sun rise tomorrow, simply because God requires no information or prayer from us. God will go about Its business of governing this universe, and in due time the sun will rise. Praying in the manner of petitioning and beseeching will not change the orderly rhythm of God's universe. God's work is done, God's laws are in operation, God's processes are already in work. That which *is*, divinely and eternally *is*, and we cannot influence God to make it so, or to prevent its being so.

This gives us quite a different concept of God than many we have entertained heretofore. We have felt that it was important and necessary that we acquaint God with our needs and the needs of the world. The Master has told us, ". . . your Father knoweth what things ye have need of, before ye ask him," and ". . . it is your Father's good pleasure to give you the kingdom." This should have taught us that the nature of prayer is a realization of the nature of God, of God's laws and God's love, and that the prayer which attempts to tell or ask God is not of much avail.

In reviewing the nature of God and the nature of prayer, you have been meditating; you have been pondering; you have been contemplating. Think on this word "contemplation" and see if you can bring your prayer to be a contemplation—an intent and grateful consideration of that which *is*. This would not be a line of thought intended to change something or hopeful of getting something; not a line of thought which would make it appear that you know more of the earth's needs than God knows, or that you have more love than God.

In this contemplative state you transcend the desire to tell God anything, or ask God for anything, and your contemplation takes the form of witnessing the sun, the moon, the stars, the tides, the growing and living things. Your contemplation takes the form of remembering that the heavens and the earth are filled with everything of which man has need. All that you behold is showing forth God's glory, God's law, God's love for His Children, and it is then that you are in a state of meditation in which the assuring words of scripture are fulfilled: "Thou wilt keep him in perfect peace, whose mind is stayed on thee"; "In all thy ways acknowledge him, and he shall direct thy paths."

This contemplation of God's Presence and Law in this universe is a simple form of meditation. It keeps your mind continuously centered in God and prevents it straying to other subjects, and yet there is no strain because you are not trying to accomplish or acquire anything. Quietly, gently and peacefully, you are observing God in action on earth as He is in heaven; you are witnessing the very glories of God. As you contemplate the glories of God that already exist and are available for your beholding, you are praising God, acknowledging God, and you are bearing witness to the fact that God's Grace is your sufficiency.

As you are engaged in this spiritual activity of

beholding God at work, day in and day out, you will be brought to a state of consciousness where thought, of its own accord, will slow down and finally stop. And one day in a second of silence the activity or Presence of God will make Itself known to you. From that moment you will know that the kingdom of God *is* within you, and no longer will you seek your good in the outer realm; no longer will you feel compelled to depend on persons or things or conditions.

Once you come to the realization that God's Grace is your sufficiency you will be living a life of continuous prayer. You will pray without ceasing, and yet never will you desire anything, nor tell God of any need, nor try to influence God to give it to you. You will be in a continuous state of prayer merely with the realization that the *Grace of God*, which has peopled this earth and filled it with all good things for man's use, *is your sufficiency in all things!* The wisdom which is God's is your sufficiency. The divine love which has met every need of this earth is your sufficiency. Could you ask more than the realization that the infinite Intelligence that governs this universe is governing your individual affairs? that the divine Love that is shown forth in the creation and maintenance of this universe is interested in your life, your business, your home? God's Grace is sufficient to fill this earth, therefore it must be sufficient for your individual needs.

The moment you know that the Grace of the Father within is your sufficiency (as well as the sufficiency of every individual being) you are forever removed from the need of human dependence, and yet it would give you love, joy, abundance, freedom, security and peace. You are forever freed from clutching at any person or any thing in the world. And the very moment that your neighbor has this same awareness there are two of you living in union with God and perfect unity with each other. When we ate in union with God we are in unity with each other, and in this unity we are at peace; we have a fellowship; we are freed of hates, envies, jealousies, malice. We want nothing that the other person has, and we are willing to share what we have, because we are receiving and accepting divine Grace. In this unity there is a relaxation from fear, doubt and distrust, and we are enabled to love and trust each other, and to have faith and confidence in each other.

Our need is the realization of the nature of God and God's government, and the contemplation of this is a form of meditation which leads to other and higher forms, and onto higher levels of consciousness. Eventually we are led to that place in consciousness where meditation is a total silence of thought, a complete state of awareness in which there is an inner alertness, an inner awakening, a state of receptivity and expectancy into which flows the realization of the Presence of God. Beyond that we need nothing. It is far better to have that realization than to have the entire world of fame and fortune at your command, because that realization is the multiplier of loaves and fishes. It makes no difference what the immediate need may be, the Presence of God is the fulfillment of that need.

At some point in this contemplation, a natural question probably will come to your mind: If it is true that God is the infinite Intelligence and the divine Love governing this universe, how do we account for the sin, disease, lack and limitation that is in the world? The answer lies in our separation, or sense of separation, from God. One of the things that has separated us from God has been our prayers. Nothing tends to separate us more than the prayers we have been taught for generations, because those prayers deny God's infinite Wisdom and deny God's infinite Love. When you ask God for something, you have declared that God is *not* the infinite Intelligence nor the divine Love, and you have separated yourself from It.

One of the Master's greatest teachings is that it is not necessary to take thought for our lives, what we shall eat or drink or how we shall be clothed, because our heavenly Father *knoweth* that we have need of these things. The nations of the world (meaning the materialistic, the ignorant and unknowing— the unspiritual) pray for these things, but not ye. "But rather seek ye the kingdom of God; and all these things shall be added unto you . . . for it is your Father's good pleasure to give you the kingdom."

The prayer that brings God into availability is not the prayer that sets itself up to know more than God. The prayer that availeth much is the realization of the true nature of God, and that prayer brings us into attunement or at-one-ment with the Presence and the Power. The prayer of petition must separate us from our good, because it is a prayer that has no knowledge of the nature of God. You do not know God aright until you know God as infinite Wisdom and divine Love. You do not know

God aright until you have the ability to cease asking.

In our ignorance we have become separated from the actual individual experience of God, and so we must ask that God reveal Itself. We must ask for wisdom, for light, for Grace, but that is all. "Ask, and it shall be given to you; seek, and ye shall find; knock, and it shall be opened unto you." Ask, again and again: "Open my eyes that I may see; open my ears that I may hear. Open my eyes of spiritual vision that I may perceive spiritually; that I may comprehend spiritually; that *I may know Thee as Thou art!*" That form of asking is wisdom, but asking for supply, security and peace is not. Supply, security and peace are free gifts to the world *now*, and they are waiting for us to avail ourselves of them by bringing ourselves into harmony with God's Law.

By the time you have contemplated God from this standpoint, and reviewed the nature of God's work on earth and realized that there *is* an infinite Wisdom and a divine Love governing this universe, there will come over you such a feeling of peace that you will wonder what you ever were concerned about. However, just stating that God is infinite Wisdom and divine Love will not do much for you. It is only as a result of this contemplation that you actually agree, from your own inner experience, that it is true. There must be the actual experience of inner awareness which comes as a result of this contemplation of God.

As you persist in this contemplation, God will become a new experience, and you will find yourself developing, or with a developed state of consciousness in which you will never look to God for anything. You will be living in the realization of God continuously flowing, and you will realize that the kingdom of God, literally, *is within you*. It is through meditation that you make contact with this kingdom, and as a result of that higher state of consciousness immediately you begin to see the greater harmonies of mind, body, purse, family and community relationships appear in your experience. It will only be necessary to rest in peace and quiet, and *let* the Grace of God fill your mind and soul, being and body, and then you will smile in the realization: Thy wisdom is sufficient for me. Thy love satisfies me; I rest in Thee.

Contemplation

"The heavens declare the glory of God: and the firmament sheweth his handywork."

When you are close to nature out in the country, in the mountains or by the sea, and more especially when in a peaceful, quiet and reflective mood, you become aware of many wonderful and beautiful things that ordinarily slip your attention and thought. Often in the evenings when I am sitting on the lanai, I become aware of the millions of stars overhead, and in contemplation of their number and brilliance have noticed the constellation known as the Southern Cross. After watching it rise and set a number of times with perfect regularity, you realize that there is a law, an order and an activity behind this event which *produces* this experience every night. And so it is also with the regular and orderly rising of the moon, the ebb and flow of the tides, the succession of growing things each in its own season.

In pondering this in connection with prayer, can you not see that it would be sinful to pray for the Southern Cross to rise in the sky, or to pray for the tide to come in or go out? Would it not be sinful to pray for flowers to bloom when all one has to do is to behold the great mystery of Life unfold, disclose and reveal Itself before your very eyes? The great prophets of old saw that man need do nothing about these great miracles except to behold them, to enjoy them, and to be grateful that there is an infinite Wisdom, a divine Love, and that *It* has created all these things for *Its own glory*. This really means for your glory and for mine, *because God's only existence is as you and as me!*

We have seen before that it is useless to pray for supply. If you were to be so practical as to think in terms of meat and potatoes, clothing, fresh air, pure water, you know that there is an over-abundance of these things in the world—there is no use praying for them. There are enough people in the world that everyone can have an abundance of companions, so there is no use praying for companionship. Certainly if God has created the heavens, the earth and the oceans, and if God has stocked the earth with all the good things, do you doubt for a moment that He created a perfect body for you, for your use, for your pleasure and expression? God could not have given us so much of His Grace, expressed in infinite supply, without also having given us perfect bodies. As you behold the orderly processes of what we call nature, and as you perceive the invisible activity of the Spirit *as It appears outwardly* as the harmonies of life, then do you see the futility of praying for anything.

If it is not necessary to pray for all of these things, what is there left to pray for? It has previously been stated that every time you resist the temptation to pray, you are in prayer. This seems a strange statement, and one you might question. At first this seems to wipe out prayer and the need for prayer, but something in your heart tells you that prayer is a glorious thing; that prayer is a necessary thing; and that prayer is one of the most beautiful experiences on earth. Something within tells you that prayer must be the very Voice of God, the very atmosphere of God, the very consciousness of God. Something tells you that prayer is a sacred and secret thing; that you must not pray to be seen of men, but that you must retire into an inner sanctuary, the secret place of the most High, and there pray in the realization that "The Lord is my shepherd." Because the Lord *is* my shepherd, the Lord's Grace is my sufficiency.

God must love His Son for He created the whole of heaven and earth for His Son—for you and for me. It is more wonderful to know that God loves me, than to know that I love God! God's Love is expressed as my love, reflected by my love, for without God's Love for me I could not love God. You can readily see that this is a two-way activity, much more so than in human experience. It is not difficult to love those who love us, but it is very difficult to love those who have little or no feeling for us. And so I am not too concerned about my love for God, because that would not exist at all except for God's Love for me. Just the realization of God's Love for His universe and for His Children is prayer, and in this prayer there are no desires that God should love me more than He does, no feeling that God should be doing more than *He already is doing*.

If there is any desire at all it is that I may more greatly appreciate God's Love and what it is doing in my life, in my mind, in my Soul, in my body and purse. It would be well to ponder more the beauties and bounties that abound on every hand, and realize that none of this would be but for the Love of God for His Children. God has given us the sun that we may have light by day; the moon that we may have light by night. He has given us the earth and the seas that we may be fed, that we may travel; He has given us soft breezes that we may be refreshed. God has provided for our every need.

Prayer is a contemplation of the beauties and bounties of God, and prayer is a contemplation of the activity of God in our experience and in the experience of the world. This prayer makes you a contemplative, and yet it does not take you out of the world. It is not necessary to leave the world to contemplate God's Grace. Just take a little time during your busy days and nights to be close to God. Go where you can see the sky, the sea or a lake, and contemplate, be in prayer, be in communion with God. You can be in prayer while engaged in any of the human activities. Whether keeping house or going to business you can reserve an area of consciousness for the contemplation of God's Presence, and you can be beholding God's

Presence in every activity going on about you. Lift your thoughts to God, open your inner ear to hear the still, small Voice, and with your inner eye behold the universe of Spirit, even while your physical eyes are engaged in physical activities. You can be in the world, but not of it.

Quickly you will understand why desire is a sin, unless the desire is for a greater realization of God, the things of God and the thoughts of God. God's thoughts are not your thoughts, and certainly your thoughts can never be God's thoughts, but *God's thoughts can become your thoughts* if you learn to contemplate God as a form of prayer, rather than to desire or even expect. Expectancy, however, can be prayer if your expectancy is that of watching the bud become the blossom; of beholding the sky suddenly filled with the light of the stars and the moon; of waiting expectantly as the sun rises and the fullness of its light and warmth envelopes you. When expectancy is that God shall move outside Its orbit to obey your directions, supplications, personal desires and wishes, then it becomes a sin.

Several years ago I said that there would never be another Infinite Way Class unless more were revealed to me on the subject of prayer. There have been many Classes since then, but each one has been a recognition that we have not yet arrived at the fullness of the understanding of prayer, and each one has been towards a higher concept of prayer. Prayer is our only contact with God, and it is only through prayer that the beauties, the activities, the abundance, the joys and peace of God's Grace can reach us. There is absolutely no way to come into or

136

under God's government other than through prayer, and when we are in prayer we are enfolded in God.

True prayer is the higher concept in which we contemplate the infinite ways that God has of *loving us*, and in which we no longer turn to God for anything except the joy of basking in His Presence, in His Grace, and in His Love. Do not be too concerned about your love for God. That will follow in a normal and natural way, and you will give expression to it. Actions speak louder than words, and it is not always those who speak much of their love who love the most. Contemplate God's Love for you, and contemplate the infinite forms of God's Love for His Creation.

In God's Love there is no criticism, no judgment and no condemnation. In God's Love there are no yesterdays. God's Love is flowing now, and It cannot withhold Itself nor can It give Itself. God's Love is a state of *is*, a state of being, and in *meditation and contemplation of God's Love* you are realizing It, feeling It, aware of It until God's Love so permeates your consciousness that you no longer pray. You are aware only of *being in prayer*.

Prayer is a contemplation of God's Love for His Kingdom. Prayer is a realization of God's Presence filling all space. Prayer is an awareness of peace, of joy and abundance. Prayer is an inner stillness and a silence, a refraining from thought and desire. Prayer is beholding and witnessing God's Grace. Prayer is a realization of *is*. Prayer is the holy contemplation that where Thou art, I am; that where I am, Thou art: "Son, thou art ever with me, and all that I have is thine." God's Grace *is* my sufficiency in all things. God's Love *is* enveloping me and this universe. God's Peace *is* upon this world. "The Lord *is* my shepherd; I shall not want." Wherever I am, the Lord *is*, even though I make my bed in hell.

Prayer is a contemplation of *is*. God *is*! Life *is*! Love *is*! Joy *is*! Prayer is an outflowing of gratitude that Thou hast given us the heavens and the earth for our glory. Prayer is a heart full of gratitude that there are still greater blessings in prayer than you have ever known or dreamed of. "Thou wilt shew me the path of life: in thy presence is fulness of joy; at thy right hand there are pleasures for evermore."

When going into prayer it is helpful to remember that we may pray for anything—as long as it is not of *this world*!

Love is the Fulfilment of the Law

"Owe no man any thing, but to love one another; for he that loveth another hath fulfilled the law. . . . Thou shalt love thy neighbor as thyself. . . . Love worketh no ill to his neighbor: therefore love is the fulfilling of the law."

Are you fulfilling the law of Love in the measure of which you are capable? If love is not fulfilling your being, you are not fulfilling the law of Love, and you have separated yourself from the fulfillment.

God is not a giving God, nor is He a withholding God. God is a state of divine being *now*, and so your life experience represents the degree in which you are fulfilling the law of Love. Any lack of demonstration, any lack of peace, harmony or security

138

represents your violation of the law of God. It represents withholding of love from your fellowman; it represents not doing unto others as you would have others do unto you. This does not necessarily mean in the line of service, although, of course, this has its rightful place. We do not so often violate the law of Love by our human conduct toward each other as by the mental concepts that we entertain. Too often we love one and dislike another; trust one and fear another, and it is in this that we violate the law of Love.

None of us would care to be judged by our degree of humanhood, because everyone falls from his own standards of what he should be. Rather would we like to be judged by what we are inside, by what we know to be our rightful Selfhood. Instead of judging by appearances, we must judge righteous judgment by looking through to the Soul of every individual and there beholding the Christ, and agreeing that there is God; there is the very Presence and Spirit of God. The Kingdom of God *is* within you, and once you discern that God is the center and circumference of every individual being (whether the individual knows or acts it or not) in that very moment you are loving your neighbor as you would want to be loved by him.

As we entertain more love of God we entertain more love of our fellowman, and we have less room in our consciousness for judgment, criticism and condemnation. We come into oneness with God in unity with man. Then it is that we are loving our neighbor as ourselves, and we are fulfilling the law of Love.

CHAPTER EIGHT

ESSENTIAL POINTS IN INFINITE
WAY PRACTICE

THE spiritual masters of old and the modern pioneers sacrificed their lives that we might have the truths that go to make up the state of consciousness that has brought us where we are today. The light that we have is the result of the light that has come down through all time. There are many whom we have no way of knowing, but there are many whom we can identify—Lao Tse, Buddha, Krishna, Shankara, Boddisattva, Jesus, John, Paul, Eckhart, Boehme, Fox, and other mystics of the twelfth to the seventeenth centuries, and the great leaders and revelators of more recent years. No one individual has given the Light to the world, but each of these great spiritual prophets has been a beam of light contributing to the Whole Light, and each has added to the mystical knowledge of the world. With this vast fund of mystical wisdom, one would think that all the earth would be free. It is strange to know that there is a God, an infinite Power of Good, and yet to witness the discords and inharmonies that still exist thousands of years after these revelations of Truth.

The Infinite Way is a modern-day unfoldment of the activity of the Spirit of God in individual consciousness; a revelation that the kingdom of heaven is on earth—now, and that the kingdom of God is within *you*!

This revelation has brought peace, harmony, healing and supply to people throughout all ages. Long before the days of Jesus, when the Christ was appearing on earth in other forms, many received this revelation, accepted it, and were enabled to demonstrate the presence and power of God in their individual experience. In every age, however, only a few benefited, while the majority continued to exist under oppression of war and slavery. At the time when the teachings of Buddha and Krishna were a light in human consciousness, a great and noble spiritual civilization existed in India, but even in that period of enlightenment there prevailed all the injustices and cruelties of the caste system. The Roman wars of the Caesars were taking place at the very time the Master was revealing the principle of Divine Love through the miracles of healing the sick, feeding the poor, and raising the dead.

Even in this present day of enlightened Christianity, when existent in the minds of men is a principle that heals the body, increases supply, and brings harmony and integrity into our individual lives, starvation of mind, body and Soul is evident on every hand. It has always been thus: a few have received the light of spiritual consciousness by being brought into contact with the Lao Tses, the Buddhas or the Jesuses that have existed throughout all ages, but the great mass of mankind has lived on the outer fringe, totally unaware that present, with them and within them, is the means of salvation.

Many students of Truth have benefited by this

light in some degree or another, and have witnessed its healing ministry, but still have not brought into their individual experience the full benefits that could be derived by a more active awakening on their part. For instance, if there were shades on all your windows, you would be in darkness, without benefit of the light and warmth of the sun. It would be foolishness to close your eyes in meditation and, upon opening them, expect the blinds to be removed. If you want the blinds removed, *it is your function to remove them!* It is useless for any student of The Infinite Way to believe that there is some kind of a miracle-working God who is going to be his private, personal and very special emissary. Spiritual wisdom reveals that the activity of Truth must take place in individual consciousness, and so there remains one thing: the individual responsibility, or the responsibility of the individual to recognize the truth, accept it, and practice it until such time as his whole life is a visible, living testimony to Truth and Grace.

In John 13:5-34, we read that the Master washed the feet of the disciples, and gave them a new commandment: "That ye love one another; as I have loved you, that we also love one another." To this day, on Maundy Thursday of each year, the reigning monarch of England commemorates this occasion by washing the feet of the poor, and giving them food and coins as a reminder that there must be a sense of humility, charity and brotherly love in the lives of all men. If you are able to see through this ceremony to the principle behind it, you will find a lesson which will be of great benefit, but only if you accept and practice it. The principle behind this holy day is that from out of our infinity we share our abundance with those who do not yet know the infinite nature of their individual being through their Christhood.

Where is this abundance from which you are to share? God is the creative Principle of all that exists. God is the Source, the Fount of all good: the measure of good is infinity, and there can be no limit to the amount of good to be shared. To the people of the world this means nothing, but to those of spiritual vision it means, "I and my Father are one; Son, thou art ever with me, and all that I have is thine." Those of spiritual vision must acknowledge that since God is the Creative Principle of all that is, creation must be infinite; since the relationship between God and His Son is oneness, you have an infinity to share. Although outwardly it may seem that you have but one dollar, in the recognition of the infinite nature of your own being you can take at least one coin and say, "Out of the visible evidence of my infinity, I will share that which I have."

On the scale of the Spirit, money is the least of that which we have to give, so let us not look to the purse to see how many dollars we have. "Silver and gold have I none; but such as I have give I thee." Turn to the infinite consciousness within and see how much of forgiveness, justice, kindness, freedom, harmony and wholeness you can bestow. Count your wealth by the realization of your Sonship with God. Every truth that has been revealed from the beginning of time is given as living scripture, to be embodied within you, lived and practiced. "I and my

Father are one. . . . All things that the Father hath are mine," does not mean anything unless you are willing to take that truth into consciousness, and practice it daily by beginning to give and to share. This is an omnipresent principle, but it will produce nothing in the way of harmony and peace unless you, as an individual, practice it.

How are students of spiritual wisdom to conduct themselves and practice this principle so that the sins, lacks, diseases and discords of the world do not enter in? The 91st Psalm promises, "He that dwelleth in the secret place of the most High shall abide under the shadow of the Almighty." The 15th Chapter of John promises, "If ye abide in me, and my words abide in you, ye shall ask what ye will, and it shall be done unto you." In both cases the responsibility is upon *your* shoulder to dwell consciously in the secret place of the most High; to abide in the Word, and let the Word abide in you. Living the spiritual life is not a matter of mere blind faith, saying, "I believe in God, so let God do it." In the spiritual life these principles must be brought actively and consciously into bearing upon your every thought. You must pray without ceasing! You must know the truth without ceasing!

Every parent or head of a household has a spiritual responsibility to the members of his household. Of course, this does not involve living their lives, since each is a free individual, each is on a different level of consciousness, and each responds to different impulses. Even within the same family it is inevitable that one will take the glorious path of uprightness, while another must take the downward path of the prodigal son. You cannot prevent one or the other, but that does not lessen your spiritual responsibility to bring to conscious remembrance every truth that you know of God, omnipresent, omnipotent, omniscient; God, infinite, good, available and practical.

Many elderly people have permitted themselves to grow old, not merely through the unfoldment of time but, through ignorance, have also taken on senility and infirmity. Far beyond the human responsibility of caring for them, yours is the spiritual responsibility of realizing that the Father and Son are one. God is the life of these dear ones, and if the Father is ageless, the Son is ageless: therefore, they have perfect life, eternal life and immortal life.

At certain seasons of the year you are confronted with epidemics of this, that and the other thing, and the world beliefs about the dangers to which your children are subjected. Frequently you hear that this or that one has a child's disease, together with the expressed hope that he will get two more so as to get them over. This is utter nonsense: none of these things can come nigh your dwelling place if you are praying without ceasing. Here it is well to remember one thing: you have no children! They are the Children of God, and God is their life, their Soul, their being. This also is true in the classroom. A teacher who has learned spiritual wisdom has a responsibility far beyond teaching A-B-Cs and 1-2-3s, and that is to realize that these are not child-minds and child-bodies, but that each is the Mind of God, disclosing and revealing Itself; each is the Temple of the living God, unfolding normally, joyfully, innocently and harmoniously.

Philosophy and religion teach that we are poor, weak mortals, and yet they acknowledge that God is our Father. Is that not a sin? God is our Father, therefore *we are divine sons*, subject only to the government of the Father! We are Children of God, and we have the infinite spiritual storehouse of the Father to draw upon for life and love, for forgiveness, justice and mercy, for integrity, loyalty and fidelity. The very Soul of God is your individual Soul, and it is out of that Soul (the kingdom of God within you) that your good flows. However, it is available only in the degree of your knowing the truth, consciously realizing it, practicing and making it a part of your own being.

Every individual who, by Grace of God, has been given one tiny bit of spiritual wisdom must practice it! The practice of spiritual wisdom is called prayer, and it is through prayer that the harmonies of God become evident in your experience. The degree of your own unfoldment depends upon how much you practice the Presence of God each day. The Presence of God is the presence of Truth, the presence of Life, the presence of harmony, the presence of wholeness. You must practice, whether on your knees scrubbing floors, or on your knees before the altar. Pray —pray without ceasing! "For unto every one that hath shall be given, and he shall have abundance." If you have more spiritual light than other members of your family, more is expected and demanded of you. This may entail awakening earlier in the morning, and consciously (I emphasize that word "consciously") realizing that the so-called laws of matter and disease are not laws—they are but human theories, beliefs and opinions. The false laws of economics which have led nations into bankruptcy are man-made laws. There is only one true law of economics—the spiritual law: the more you give, the more you have.

God is Spirit. God is infinite. Therefore, Spirit is infinite, and Spirit is all there is. Spiritual law is the only law. Spiritual life is the only life. Spiritual intelligence is the only wisdom. Spiritual guidance is the only guidance. However true this may be, it will not help you or your families to the degree that it should unless you, yourself, embody this truth. Outwardly, the spiritual life will appear to be a way of doing nothing: inwardly, it is a way of constant spiritual activity in consciousness; a continuous knowing of the truth. Harmony is brought into your experience in proportion as this truth is active in your consciousness.

You may wonder if there is never a rest from this. I can assure you that in the twenty-five years of my study and practice there has been no end to it. Instead, the activity seems to increase with each day. From the moment that you begin to consciously know the truth and permit truth to be active in your consciousness, you will find yourself being called upon by relatives and friends, and even by strangers who perceive that you have something of which they have need. Family life will always be your first consideration, but in addition to all the truth you must know for them, it will also be necessary to know a little more for those who come to you. This practice compels you to dwell in the secret place of the most High for even longer periods and, in its turn, draws still more unto you, and this wheel within a wheel continues until you find yourself being drawn upon from all quarters. For the person on the spiritual Path there is no such thing as day or night, no such thing as a holiday. Every minute of every day belongs to God, and you may be called upon any hour of the twenty-four, any day of the seven.

The demonstration of spiritual principles calls for steadfastness in devotion and purpose. Since God is the only law and the only law-giver, it naturally follows that the only law operating in human consciousness is spiritual law. Even though it has been brought to your attention repeatedly that there is no law of disease, no law of sin, no law of lack, it does not mean that instantly you will be free of all discords. It means that each time you are tempted to experience such discords in your own life or the lives of those who look to you, you will be called upon to stand fast in your realization that it exists only as an appearance, and that it is not happening in Reality: because God alone is Truth, and Spirit alone is Reality there is no law to sustain it. There will be times, when confronted with some appearance of great need, that you will be inclined to discouragement, but that is not the way of the Spirit. Jesus was tempted at every step on His journey, and even when the devil left Him, he left only for a season: always the tempter returned, in one form or another, until finally, at Gethsemane and on Calvary, the Master was faced with the temptation to believe that even God had forsaken Him. While to appearances it would seem that mounting a cross to be crucified meant an absence of God or a lack of demonstration, nevertheless in the steadfastness of His own realization that "I and my Father are one," there could be no absence of God.

As you rise higher in spiritual Grace, more and more temptations (not less) will come to you. However, the day finally comes when you will be so lifted in consciousness that you realize you could live the rest of your days without a single problem. But there is the world of family and friends, and as long as this is so you cannot escape their problems. You may arrive at the consciousness of peace, but still you will be tempted to believe that the rest of the world is in the tomb of human existence.

Rising out of the tomb to all forms of human existence is possible, but possible only in proportion to what you put into the attempt. If you wished to explore an unknown country or to make a million dollars, you know the sacrifices you would be called upon to make, because you know the sacrifices others have made in attaining fame and fortune. You want health and supply, you want peace and joy, you want life everlasting, and so you must sacrifice sloth, indolence, laziness and indifference. You must begin to know the truth today, and know it and know it and know it! Each day of not knowing the truth postpones the day of salvation.

At the earliest moment of the morning, and continuously during the day, become aware of every spiritual truth that you can bring to remembrance, and as you go about your duties always keep in consciousness some spiritual truth which is the law to your family and your affairs. Wonderful truths are to be found in all the scriptures of the world, and no one should be without some statement that can be pondered in thought and applied throughout the day. As you become more proficient in this practice, the errors of your own household are dispelled, and, if you continue on the spiritual Path, eventually the day will come when you will have patients and students, and you will find that your responsibility extends farther than your own household. Then it is that you must be willing to lay down your life, and that means you must be willing to lay down your comfort, your rest and your time. You must be willing to hew to the line twenty-four hours of each day in order that others may receive the light that you, yourself, have been given through the Grace of God.

Each one who receives some measure of spiritual light must let that light shine—in his own life, in his household, in his community. No one has the right to avoid this, and in the end no one will have the ability to avoid it. Just as the lighthouse is for the benefit of the ships that pass by, so are ye the light of the world, that those not yet aware of their true identity may be lighted on their way.

SELF-COMPLETENESS IN GOD
Finding the Answers to "Problems"

The practice of spiritual wisdom must be applied to all the experiences of daily living—the minor as well as the major ones. Each day we are faced with so-called problems which are but temptations to believe in a selfhood apart from God, and as these temptations come to take thought for some outer condition we find ourselves in a quandary: What shall I do about this, and how shall I go about that? When called upon to do something exceeding our present financial, mental or physical capacity, we are immediately inclined to start thinking, planning, hoping and despairing, and to say, "It cannot be done; it is an impossibility."

The simple application of spiritual wisdom is to realize that the answer lies within you—not in your mental or physical capacity, but in the Christ of your being. You are Self-complete in God. The kingdom of God, the all-ness of God is within you, and you can turn there for the answer to every problem. Every detail of your life is already complete and established, way down deep in consciousness, and there is no problem so involved or so enormous that the answer does not lie within you.

Instead of striving externally for the answer, on the basis of your Self-completeness in God, go within, and the answer will appear: you will be led, guided and directed. Even if you were lost in the wilderness, you would be led to safety through your realization that the kingdom of God within you is infinite, full and complete; forever flowing forth, revealing and disclosing Itself to your humanhood.

As you continue the practice of spiritual wisdom, you learn to withdraw your dependence on outside avenues, and soon you will find that it is literally true —*you are self-complete*. Although the answer sometimes comes *through* some person, circumstance or condition in the external realm, it does not come *from* them—it comes from the depths of your own being.

Believe in your Self-completeness in God. Believe that you can turn to the kingdom of God within you for any answer, any supply, any love, any wisdom—for anything necessary in your experience. Believe that you can turn within and receive the assurance of God's Presence, and then watch your good appear in the without. "In returning and rest shall ye be saved; in quietness and in confidence shall be your strength."

The Divine Author

The discords and inharmonies of human experience are caused by the state of mesmerism that binds us to the world of appearances. If we judge life from the standpoint of what we behold with the five physical senses, we are hypnotized to the world of appearances, and are thereby in bondage to person, place and thing. As we become de-hypnotized so that we do not judge by appearances, we find an entirely different situation.

Looking at life and the world as it appears to be, when an individual's particular avenue or channel of income or supply is suddenly cut off, we may feel apprehensive, and wonder where his next income or supply will come from. Again we look to our illustration of the tree: regardless of how bare of leaves and flowers and fruit the branches may seem, our higher intelligence beholds that in the ground, in the roots, in the tree, a law is at work; and in due time the leaves, the flowers and the fruit will appear. This is not by any virtue of the tree, nor of the ground or the roots, but by virtue of the infinite invisible law of life which functions inside and outside the tree.

This invisible law operates to bring moisture and minerals and the substances of the earth to the tree, and to attract to it everything necessary for its development.

Let us pretend that we are at the theater, and as we follow the performance we become fearful that the villain in the piece will harm the hero and the heroine in the next act. However, if we are theater-wise we will not be concerned about the villain, since we know that there is a greater authority—that is, the author of the play—and that the author, and the idea of the play in the consciousness of the author, determines how the villain will act and what will happen to the rest of the cast. The villain, in and of himself, can do nothing to the hero or the heroine, nor to the action of the play; and even the good characters cannot be good, any more than the evil characters can be evil. Throughout the play, the determining influence is the mind of the author. Once this is established in thought, we do not look to the players for anything except the excellence of their performance, since the idea and plot of the play is the activity of the mind of the author, expressed through the characters on stage.

We must learn to adopt this method of looking at life. Instead of fearing what this person or that circumstance or situation can do to us, and instead of becoming overly excited about the good which this or that one may bring about in our experience, we must learn to look behind the scenes to the Infinite Invisible, which is the Mind of the Author, God. God is the author and finisher of our world, of our work, and of our lives, and if we look to

God, the one Mind, the infinite Intelligence and the divine Love of the universe, we will find that regardless of what any individual or group of individuals may appear to be doing at any given moment, in the final analysis, the decision rests with God.

Since God is the mind of individual man, it follows that man can carry out only the lines given him by the great Author of the universe. Since the nature of that Mind is love, truth, principle, it necessarily follows that only such qualities and such activities can become a part of our universe. It is true, however, that many people do not know that they receive their lines direct from the Author, and they are unaware that they are but vehicles for carrying out the divine plot. These people have set up the words "I", "me", "mine", and they live out from the basis of "I", "me", and "mine", and thereby ultimately bring themselves to disaster. The only reason for error in any form is due to the belief of an "I" or a selfhood apart from God. This false sense of "I", with its need to supply, support and maintain itself, plan and do for itself (and not having the wisdom or the power to do so) has produced every discord and inharmony. The restoration of harmony comes with the giving up of this false sense of "I" through the realization that God is the only Selfhood, the only Life, Principle, Power, Substance and Being of all that is. No one can write his own part: it takes the Mind of the great Author to plan and to direct, and as we become obedient to that direction we find our lives God-governed, harmoniously maintained and sustained.

Here the question arises: Cannot those who do not recognize God-government, and who do not bring themselves under the divine law, influence our experience and hinder our demonstration? The answer is: No, they cannot! As we, individually, look to God as the author and finisher of our world, and as we steadfastly hold to the truth that "the government shall be upon his shoulder," we come to understand that the visible scene is but the idea of God made manifest, the plan and work of the great Author made visible as our individual experience. Through this resolute holding to the truth, those who become a part of our experience as family, friends or fellow-citizens, either become healed and take their normal and natural places in our lives, or they are removed from the range of our experience where they can have no further influence upon the harmony of our existence.

It is not possible to heal all who come within range of our thought, since there must be a preparedness and a willingness for healing. The Master did not heal Judas, and eventually he destroyed himself. But Judas did not bring about the death of the Master, because He survived the experience. Even the Master could not prevent Peter's denials, but in that case there was a healing. It becomes necessary for us to break the sense of mesmerism that holds us in the belief that persons or circumstances, in and of themselves, have power or jurisdiction over our affairs; rather, in the face of every appearance, we must hold to the truth that only the Infinite Invisible governs, controls, supports, maintains and sustains. The Infinite Invisible, acting as man and circumstances, helps us to play our part in the drama of life.

God, the Infinite Invisible, is the creative principle of this universe, and this universe "sheweth his handywork." God's handywork shows forth divine law and order; it shows forth the loving qualities and the spiritual activities; but this is shown forth in our experience only in proportion as we understand that the people and things and situations of this world are but vehicles for the operation of the Infinite Invisible, and that, in and of themselves, they do not have power. Every character in the drama of life is showing forth the activity of the Author, and no character and no situation contains any element not given it by the Author, and therefore the play must end as the Author has planned it.

Your attention has previously been brought to the fact that mesmerism, or hypnotic suggestion, is really the one evil, and it is that which would make you look at person, place, thing, circumstance and condition, and have you believe that the issues of life abide in these. Whereas, spiritual wisdom, spiritual intelligence and spiritual intuition would have you realize and know that person, place, thing, circumstance or condition are but the vehicles for the unfoldment and carrying out of the divine plan as it has been understood in the Mind which is God. In this understanding, we will not look to any person for our satisfaction, companionship or supply, but rather, we will understand that whoever is playing that part in our experience at this moment is really carrying out the divine activity of love and life, and if, for any reason, these should be removed, the Author has already provided another player for that part. Should we find any door of supply or opportunity closed to us, we will understand that it is the activity of the Mind of the Author operating for the good of the entire play, therefore that same Mind has provided another source, another avenue or channel for us.

As we emerge from the mesmerism of the world, we come into greater enjoyment of the visible scene, knowing that, unknown to the senses and hidden from the eye, is the Infinite Invisible, the divine Source, the great Architect and Author of the universe. As strange as it may seem, every unpleasant person or experience plays a part in our lives, but this we will not understand until we have learned not to judge by appearances, and not to become unduly elated or depressed by the outer picture. Enjoy every experience, enjoy the love of family and friends, enjoy the beauties of nature—always being conscious of the Infinite Invisible as the Source of this good, always remembering that it is the activity of the Infinite Invisible that is appearing to you as this good. When you meet with experiences of love and kindness, justice and benevolence, always remember that it is the activity of the divine Mind that is appearing to you as these experiences. Whenever you meet with negative experiences, always remember that these can exist only in the belief that the power lies within the person or circumstance. As you correct this belief within you, and understand that no individual and no circumstance and no condition has such power over you, in that proportion do you become free of the discord and in harmony.

When the Master stood before Pilate and was asked, "Knowest thou not that I have power to crucify thee, and have power to release thee?" the answer was, "Thou couldest have no power at all against me, except it were given thee from above...." This was the Master's recognition that power does not lie with man, but with God. Whenever these experiences of inharmony and discord appear, it becomes necessary to know that only the lines written in by the great Author have power, and that any lines or parts or actions not placed there by the great Author are not power, have no means of maintaining or sustaining themselves, and can have no effect upon your experience.

Whenever you stand before Pilate, always remember that there is only one "I"—God—and only the activity of God can be brought into your experience and into fruition. No claim of an "I" apart from God can maintain itself, do anything, be anything, or cause anything; nor can there be any effect from any "I" other than that "I" which is God. Your reliance on spiritual government is the realization that the Infinite Invisible is the Source of all harmony, all good—omnipresent, omnipotent, omniscient. Any thing or any person claiming to exist by virtue of an "I" or a selfhood apart from God is not power, is not presence, is not reality, is not cause, and, therefore, can produce no effect.

All that takes place in your experience is for the showing forth of God, and it is God revealing Its harmonies, Its powers, Its beauties and Its completeness, so there need be no concern for any one

or any thing or any result. It is not your understanding, your power, or your wisdom that is necessary, but the knowledge that all effect is God's
ability, God's responsibility, God's government and
God's Grace. Can you doubt that?

Freedom—by Grace

Heretofore we have been concerned with human
freedom—that is, freedom of speech, freedom of the
press, freedom of religion, economic freedom, bodily
freedom. I speak to you of spiritual freedom.

What is freedom? Freedom is Life living Itself.
Freedom is joy and peace. Freedom is the song of
the Soul, the dream of the dreamer. Freedom is
being. The man whose being is in Christ is free. I am
free and you are free, but not while we are attached
to the wheel of human thought; not while we are in
obedience to man-made government of the Soul.

Freedom is not a condition of government—freedom is a condition of the Soul. Men in chains have
been free; men have been free under slavery and
oppression. Men have prospered in periods of de-
pression and panic; men have survived war and
flood and famine. When the Soul of man is free It
carries him through Red Seas and desert experiences to the Promised Land of spiritual peace. As
we turn to the kingdom of our inner Self, we find
the reign of divine power in the outer world. As we
seek peace within, we find harmony without. As we
find freedom of the Soul, we experience the freedom
of Grace.

What prevents us from living in the highest realm
of harmony, health and abundance? What prevents

us from enjoying all the good that may be found on earth? Is there any power decreeing and enforcing poverty, disease and death? Is there any law of lack and limitation binding us to the wheel of slavery, hard labor and trial? If so, from whence do they emanate?

The world has ever sought for freedom, peace and plenty, but this search has been chiefly in the feverish activity of the human mind, in the tiring energy of brain-racked thought. The human mind, falsely educated through the centuries contains within itself all the fears and failures of the human race. All the anguish of passion, greed, lust, ambition, fear and domination is found in human thought, and there is run the race for lawless possession and voracious acquisition. The result is not freedom, but enslavement to the senses.

If one suddenly decided to withdraw from this struggle for freedom through mortal thinking, would not some unseen, unknown Power reveal Itself to human thought, and unfold without strife the infinite abundance and presence of that Bread which cometh down from heaven, satisfying all mental, physical and financial needs? With the limitation of mortal thought removed, may man not find in the enlarged vision of fearless, unfettered being, the freedom of the race? Where but in the realm of this greater understanding may man find the infinity of his good? Where but in the broad consciousness of his immortal being can the individual find his thirst slaked by the Water that will forever end the thirst for water that does not satisfy? Where but in the realm of his new consciousness can be found the

Meat that ends the hard hunger of unsatisfied desires, and frees the mind from the dizzying influence of the senses?

Freedom is a quality of thought and condition, experienced only when attachment to the manifest realm is broken. Above and beyond the lure of mortal sense is the life divine, where one enters into one's heritage of freedom. This is freedom to live in the world, and yet to be free from bondage to its attractions; to enjoy friendships, but not to be dependent upon them; to welcome money for the things it will buy, but not to be avaricious; to work, not merely to earn a living, but for the joy of it. To seek to raise the standard of our work, or to find a better way of doing the work at hand, brings freedom from drudgery, and eventually freedom from lack and limitation. To love our families and not be dismayed by their failings or too proud of their achievements; to stand back of the world and watch its comings and goings, its successes and failures, its loves and hates, and not be overcome or involved—this is freedom.

CHAPTER NINE

THE DEEP POOL OF YOUR BEING

It is well, at this point of our spiritual unfoldment, that we stop for a moment and take stock of ourselves. Just what is the *specific principle* we are trying to prove, and from which we expect great things? First of all, the principle is that God is individual consciousness; God is the consciousness of the individual; God is your consciousness and mine. Many facets of this principle have been presented in the Message, but one point, above all, that may be called the vision of The Infinite Way, and from which proceeds all else, is the principle that God is individual consciousness—be it human, animal, vegetable or mineral, God is the consciousness thereof.

Scripturally this is revealed in such passages as, "I and my Father are one; I will never leave thee, nor forsake thee; Son, thou art ever with me, and all that I have is thine." When you understand that "I" is God, you come into the understanding that God, the Infinite Intelligence of this universe, is *your* individual Mind, Life, Soul, Being, Spirit, Truth and Consciousness. That "I", which is Divine Consciousness, is wherever you are, and there is no way of escaping It. "Whither shall I go from thy spirit, or whither shall I flee from thy presence?"

This point must be very clear, because now it is

revealed that, ". . . the hour cometh, when ye shall neither in this mountain, nor yet at Jerusalem, worship the Father. . . . God is a Spirit: and they that worship him must worship him in spirit and in truth." "The kingdom of God is within you"—there is no need to seek a holy place. "The place where thou standest is holy ground"—right where *you are* is your abiding place in heaven.

All attention is centered on the kingdom of God, within you, and there is nothing to fear, even in hell, because this Divine Consciousness, or God, is your healing, protecting, sustaining and maintaining influence. Although we use terms such as healing and protection, they are not literally true, since in this realization there would be nothing to heal or from which to be protected, except the erroneous belief that you are a human being set off by yourself and in some way out of contact with God. God is your own being, and therefore *the infinite nature of God's being is the infinite nature of your own individual being.* This forever separates us from any sense of reaching out to a God somewhere, and prevents us from fearing powers "out there." It matters not whether it is something physical, mental, moral or financial, "there shall in no wise enter into it (God-consciousness, which is your individual being) anything that defileth, neither whatsoever worketh abomination, or maketh a lie."

This is absolute and complete Truth—the Truth the saints and sages have tried to reveal to human consciousness throughout the centuries. But one thing has prevented the world from accepting and living this consciousness, and it is this point: whereas all of this is true, it is of no avail to anyone except in proportion as he attains an inner realization of it. The things of God are foolishness with man, and so all of this Truth is foolishness so far as we, as human beings, are concerned, and is of no avail to us. It becomes of avail and becomes the life of your life only when you have attained that first spark of inner illumination which reveals that this is the Truth.

If you were to stand before Jesus Christ, the only reason you could be sure of an instantaneous healing is that He had attained more of this realization than you had. The only reason you can go to a spiritual healer for help today is that he has attained a greater realization of the truth of your *true identity* than you have attained. But you can go and do likewise as soon as you have arrived at some measure of that same realization. If, individually and as groups, we were sufficiently able to live with this Truth, in silent meditation and receptivity, the history of the world could be changed by the peace, the harmony, the healings and the successes that would come out of *the united silent consciousness* of "two or three gathered together in my name." One moment of the silence that thunders in Godly language is heaven, and out of that silence an infinity of healings can take place. Wherever one is desperately reaching out for a realization of the Christ or for the help of God, that one could tune-in to that silence and find peace. This silence, which has such tremendous power, is the consciousness of God when the human sense is still; when the human mind is not thinking, not trying to make a demonstration, to get or to achieve something. When the human mind is still, the Divine Mind is in active expression in the entire universe.

"The kingdom of God is within you," and there is a center of your being which is like a deep, silent pool of contentment—a deep well of silent Spirit. When you are at that center you have found heaven, and it is out of that deep inner silence, which the Master called "My peace," that the healings and harmonies and joys flow forth, and all those who have tuned-in to that Consciousness receive the benefit of It.

Let each one realize that God is individual consciousness, and that the Presence and Power of the Godhead can be brought to bear in your families, your communities, and in your nations, in proportion as you can settle back into this silence *and let it come through!* This is a difficult thing to achieve, and an individual setting about to accomplish it alone may have to go through months and sometimes years of work and meditation. My own experience required months and months of constant and persistent meditation, day and night, before I received the first second of realization, and all that time the question was: How do I know there is such a thing, and that it will accomplish anything? To my knowledge, no one had gone that way before, no one had prepared the ground, and I had no knowledge of it at all—only a conviction, an inner conviction that if I could just touch the center within myself, which is God, that that would release It into expression, and It would take over my life and the lives of those who looked to me for help. Even after the first glimpse of realization it was weeks before the second occurred, but gradually it became my entire life-experience until now it is literally true that "the words that I speak unto you I speak not of myself: but the Father that dwelleth in me, he doeth the works."

Twenty-five years of this inner meditation and contact makes it a simple thing for me to lift those who come to me so that they also can achieve it. The many chapters in the *Infinite Way Writings* devoted to "Meditation" and "Communion," and the consciousness that went into their production, makes it easier for students to achieve this peace of inner silence, and the united meditations and consciousness of our students make it easier for the rest of the world to achieve conscious communion. One by one, students are attaining a measure of ability to touch that center of their own being and get a response to it. Ultimately, the time will come when every one will be able to touch this center of his own being, at will, and find God's Power and God's Grace flowing from him into the world as an atmosphere of harmony and healing, of peace and joy to all whom he meets.

More and more, the word "meditation" is appearing in current literature, and more and more you read: Meditation—meditation is the way. Do not be misled by any of these articles. Meditation, in and of itself, is not the way! *The way is contact!* Meditation is only a way to achieve an inner silence in which the contact is made. Meditation is the way to get back into yourself, to that deep well of contentment at the center of your being, which is God, and where the personal sense of "I" disappears.

When your meditation results in contact the way has been found to let "the imprisoned splendor" escape, and only then do you understand Paul when he says, "I live; yet not I, but Christ liveth in me."

The first step in reaching this center of your being is refraining from the use of the word "I". How foolish it is to associate the personal "I" with anything having to do with God, because it is utterly impossible for an individual to be any kind of a contributing factor toward the Presence and Power of God. As a matter of fact, the opposite is true: only in proportion as you can nullify this sense of "I" can God-consciousness take over and fulfill Itself. To some extent, the word "I" has been excluded insofar as it applies to prayer or treatment: no longer would you use prayer as a means toward influencing God in any manner. Since God does not deal in material thoughts or things it is of no use to have a material wish or desire or hope. When you have learned to go to God with no desires you have eliminated the word "I", and that, in itself, is one of the biggest steps you will ever be called upon to take. In going to God you are going only for a spiritual blessing and benediction, and until you stand in the Presence of God you have no way of knowing the nature of the spiritual kingdom and its blessings. "Eye hath not seen, nor ear heard, neither have entered into the heart of men, the things which God hath prepared for them that love him. But God hath revealed them unto us by his Spirit: for the Spirit searcheth all things, yea, the deep things of God."

Through the blessings of God you are released

from the thoughts and the things of this world, and only in this release are God's blessings known and made manifest, but never in the sense of anything acquired or received from God. In no way are you taken out of the world—you are in the world, but not of it. You have found heaven, and you are free, and it is then that you begin to understand the profound significance and poetry of "My peace, still waters, green pastures." ". . . for we know not what we should pray for as we ought: but the Spirit itself maketh intercession for us with groanings which cannot be uttered."

Until the moment of contact we do not know the nature of living in a spiritual world, nor do we know the nature of a spiritual blessing. Certainly we can conceive of it, but even at our stage of development most of us are just one step ahead of the orthodox world which looks upon God as pouring out material blessings in the way of increased supply or health or happiness. God does not operate that way: those are the added things that appear in our human world *when we have been released from the thoughts and things of this world.* By just *letting* the Spirit of God work Its wonders within us, we would come into a state of consciousness in which we would find that the bounties of this world are as free and abundant as leaves on the trees, without taking any thought about them. But any sense of the personal selfhood, such as the use of "my" understanding, "my" spirituality, "my" integrity, would block or end the demonstration of spiritual good. Spirituality, understanding and integrity are the Grace of God, individually expressed, in proportion as there is no personal sense of selfhood to block it. Your part is to "die daily," and then as the Grace of God is manifest as your individual experience you witness the multiplication of the loaves and fishes, the healing of the sick, the raising of the dead. Had the Master not been able to step aside sufficiently to know that "I can of mine own self do nothing," and had the word "I" entered His demonstration in any way, the miracles could not have taken place.

This brings us back to our first point: *God* is individual consciousness (the consciousness of you and me) and therefore the storehouse of infinity is within you. You cannot draw it forth—you can get out of the way, make the contact, *and let it flow forth!* In order to understand this properly it is necessary that you first overcome time and space. You must remember that none of this has anything to do with yesterday. None of yesterday's virtues will help you achieve this realization today, and none of yesterday's sins will prevent proving it today. Your yesterday's, whether for good or evil, have nothing to do with today's spiritual unfoldment. You must rise in consciousness above any sense of limitation, and each time you turn to the within in an earnest sense of self-forgiveness and Self-realization the yesterdays are blotted out. "Though your sins be as scarlet, they shall be as white as snow," and because the nature of the Christ is forgiveness, until seventy times seven, even were you to sin again you will be "as white as snow" the moment you return. As long as you earnestly and sincerely follow this path for the purpose of "forgetting those things which are behind, and reaching forth unto those things which are before," and ". . . press toward the mark for the prize of the high calling of God in Christ Jesus," even though mistakes cling and must be risen above again and again, nevertheless there will come that day of complete attainment when there will be no going back to the yesterdays.

You do not live on yesterday's manna. It is necessary that you make this contact almost hourly throughout each day until that glorious moment when It takes over and says, "I am with you," and eventually on to the end of the road where It says, "I am you." Until that day comes your life is a continuity of Christ-experience—every day you must go to the storehouse for fresh manna. Day by day the manna fell, but always there was a Moses to turn to the inner kingdom to bring forth that manna. Day by day the Christ healed, but there was a Jesus to turn within to loose those spiritual powers. Great blessings are coming into the world today, but day by day there are those who are learning to turn within to bring forth these blessings. *God* is your storehouse of good. God is your individual consciousness; therefore, your *individual consciousness is your storehouse of good*. Many, many times each day you learn to make your contact with that infinite storehouse at the center of your being *and let it flow*, with no concern as to the form in which it will appear in your experience.

In the same way that there are no yesterdays, there are no tomorrows. Tomorrow, when it comes, is today. Right where you are in this second of consciousness, today, is the only place you can be, and this is the only time you can be. You cannot accomplish this second of consciousness yesterday or even an hour ago; you cannot accomplish it tomorrow. This can be lived only in the very second in which you find yourself, here and now. There is never any time when you can experience anything other than this second. And it is up to you *to make each second* what this second is, in the same way that you have made this second *what this second is*—by a turning within to your Source. There is no difference between the flow of God this minute or a hundred years from now—it is just a matter of continuity of the contact. The Life of God will never end, and although we cannot remain here one minute after the call has come to labor in other vineyards, as long as there is a work for us on this plane of existence we can maintain ourselves here by this contact, and maintain ourselves in all the vitality of strength, youth, health and wholeness. But we can only do it by the contact, because It is the Presence and Power that does the work.

"There's a divinity that shapes our ends," and, since this is literally true, the question arises: Why does it not do so? The answer lies in the fact that we do not make our contact with that divinity, because when we do, It brings forth whatever it is that we are to do in life. If the Finger of God touched you, It could (if that were Its Will) take you out of wherever you are and put you into a completely different life and existence, and the past would fade away. My own experience has witnessed three entirely different lives—as a business man, a healer, and now as a teacher and author of spiritual Truth,

171

but I, personally, could never have brought any of these about.

We are not all intended to be the same thing: there must be men of business and science, engineers and builders, teachers and artists—and it is the Infinite Intelligence at the center of your own being that determines your particular expression; but you will never know it unless you make the contact. In the words of Paul: "For to one is given by the Spirit the word of wisdom; to another the word of knowledge by the same Spirit; to another faith . . . to another the gifts of healing . . . to another the working of miracles; to another prophecy; to another discerning of spirits; to another divers kinds of tongues; to another the interpretation of tongues: But all these worketh that one and the self-same Spirit, dividing to every man severally as he will." There are those, however, who, by Grace of God, have made that contact without any directed effort or conscious activity on their part. Those are they who already are artists, teachers, composers, writers, one thing and another. They have made contact with their Source and are in their rightful places, but even they can increase and improve the quality and character of their output by a greater degree of conscious contact and union with their Source.

The way of this work is not to influence anyone to follow it, or try to carry it to the world at large. The way is to be joyous and free in sharing it with those who, by their eagerness and desire and willingness to sacrifice, indicate that this is a way toward which they have been led. Although thousands of people can become interested, when it comes right down to the individual sacrifice necessary to achieve this inner realization, the numbers rapidly diminish. But you can be assured that since God is your individual consciousness, with faithfulness, persistence and perseverance, you can reach the kingdom of God that is within you, and in this contact It flows forth into your experience and takes over your entire life-experience—Mind, Spirit, Soul, body, business, home—undertakings of any nature.

Consciousness Expresses Itself

From the days when man was limited to travel by foot, to this present day when the only restriction is a six-hundred-mile-an-hour jet-plane, there has been an activity of God at work in human consciousness to free man from the limitations of time and space. Man cannot hasten the day, nor can he retard it, because it is an activity of unfolding consciousness. Those who try to hold It back are destroyed, and those who are Its willing instruments are in tune with the Infinite.

This evolutionary process, which is the activity of God, unfolding, disclosing and revealing Itself, applies to our individual lives. If we are willing instruments and open ourselves, through meditation, we permit this activity of the Spirit to take over our Mind, Soul and body. If we block It by personal sense, personal will and personal desire, It breaks us. Most men of ambition end up on Elba, because the force of God destroys them; whereas, a conscious realization of that same force of God would lift them to the very heights of world recognition.

Throughout the history of the world, wars and oppression and slavery have been brought about by the failure of men to perceive the nature of God in consciousness. Freedom is never gained through war or aggression, but only by an unfolding consciousness which is taking place all over the world. There is a force greater than man, opening out Its Hand and setting all peoples free. *We are merely instruments of that unfolding consciousness.*

In this present era, the world is wondering and speculating much about life on other planets, and in this connection there is one thing that we must remember: God fills all space; there is no place where God is not. If there are other stars or planets in this universe, they were made by God, and therefore they must be embraced in God-consciousness, and they must manifest life, although there may be different degrees and forms of life. Were you to go back three or four thousand years what different forms and expressions of life, what different degrees of culture and civilization would be found! There can be no question that on other planets or spaces there is Life. There must be, because *God is*, and wherever God is. Life is, *because God is life!* As there cannot be a vacuumed life, there must be an expressed life, and that expressed life again would be individual forms of life.

Eventually, we may find that in these outer reaches of space there are civilizations as backward as was the earth several thousand years ago, or we may find them advanced thousands of years beyond where we are now. We have no way of knowing anything about that, but we do know this:

Consciousness is God, Consciousness is Life, Consciousness is that which is formed—therefore, *wherever God is, there is life!* Time and space are filled with God, and whatever forms of consciousness exist, whether behind or ahead of us, are determined by things over which we have no control, because Consciousness is forever expressing Itself.

The degree of experienced life is in proportion to the degree of consciousness unfolding. Regardless of where you are at this moment in life, that represents your degree of God-life, expressed and unfolded into conscious expression. This you can change at any time by opening out your consciousness for a greater flow. There are no yesterdays and there will be no tomorrows. There is only this instant in which you recognize that there is an activity of God operating in human consciousness, and that you are merely an instrument for Its operation and expression, and it is through your frequent periods of meditation, communion and contact that you permit It to have sway.

Effective Prayer

Only those who experience a deep, inner spiritual contact or realization can pray effectively. This may, at first, seem a shocking statement to those who have been brought up in the old teachings that we must turn to God, pray to God, ask, beseech God for this, that and the other thing. However, as we meditate and ponder this subject of effective prayer, we find that if we do not receive what we pray for, we pray amiss. Certainly we are all well acquainted with the sort of prayer that is "praying amiss."

In *The 1954 Infinite Way Letters*[1] we find this quotation: "Prayer is a spontaneous unfoldment of Truth from within our own being. Prayer is a spontaneous revelation of God in action. Prayer is our degree of receptivity to Truth. Prayer is the avenue opened within ourselves to receive the Love, Life, Truth, and the unfolding Wisdom of God."

"Prayer, then, is the spontaneous flow from the Father within, to our outer consciousness. Prayer is the recognition of the nature of God as fulfillment. Prayer is the realization of our inseparability from God. 'I and my Father are one,' is the relationship established in the beginning. One-ness with God is the divine state of our being, but only prayer can reveal it."

Why is it then that only individuals with deep spiritual realization can pray effectively? To understand this it is first necessary that we understand something of the nature of God and, through this, the nature of prayer. Through different states and stages of development we have been taught various concepts about the nature of God and the nature of prayer, but suddenly we come to a point in our experience where we realize that no longer will any of these concepts suffice. We come face to face with the realization that nothing has been given us on the nature of God or the nature of prayer that is of any value whatever in this particular moment; and it is then that we must begin to strip away the centuries of false beliefs and ideas that have built up in our consciousness through being subjected to the world's concepts concerning these two great points.

[1] By Joel S. Goldsmith.

176

No one can tell us anything about the nature of God or the nature of prayer. We come to realize that no matter what we knew yesterday or this morning —in fact, if the realization we had at those times would literally raise the dead, *now* we must be renewed. In this moment we must come to a deeper realization of the nature of God and the nature of prayer, and as we go within our own consciousness we realize that we must give up any idea that there is a God to whom we can pray; that there is any God who can be cajoled, wheedled or influenced to bring about any personal desire, or desired effect.

We must consider carefully all of the different concepts that have pressed in upon us. It is true that at certain stages of our development we have been taught to pray for things, for ideas, and then for spiritual realization, and there was nothing wrong with those prayers at that particular time. But now, today, this very minute in this moment in eternity, none of the old ideas or concepts are of any avail, and they must be weeded out and cast from us. As we turn within in stillness and in silence, with an utter lack of old conceptual beliefs and old ideas, we begin to realize, even in a small measure, the fact that there is a God that is "Closer than breathing, nearer than hands and feet"; and that we live and move and have our being in that Infinite, Invisible Spirit. We become conscious of it the moment that no old ideas or concepts, no desires or wishings interfere with the listening that is going on within us.

As we sit in this silence, listening, attentive, waiting for the Word of God to well up in us, we find a new dimension coming into our experience regarding

God, the nature of God and the nature of prayer. Surely this experience is prayer in a sense that is more real, more definite than any we have heretofore known; surely in this moment we are developing to a higher degree that inner listening ear that is the reality of communion. And so in this stillness, in this lack of mental and physical effort, in this moment of peacefulness, of letting go, of relaxing, we reach that point at the center of our being, and make contact with the Infinite Invisible that is within us. It is then that a transformation takes place, be it great or small in our eyes, and where once there was concept, erroneous concept, now there is, in some degree, knowledge of reality—calm, confident, serene knowledge in the realization of the nature, the activity, the essence and the being of that which we call God. In this moment of contact, in some small measure we have really, truly, experienced God, and it is this experience and this alone that constitutes effective prayer.

Only in the depths of an inner contact within the consciousness of an individual who has been sufficiently attuned to this Infinite within can one arrive at effective prayer. Only in the degree in which we, as individual consciousness, lose ourselves and become one in conscious awareness of the Infinite Invisible within us, are we able spiritually to transcend, to see through the things in our experience. There is no other type of effective prayer as we know it. The reason the prayers of saints and sages and practitioners seem more effective than ours is that they, through Grace, and through a process of inner development, have arrived at a state of spiritual consciousness which permits of constant, continuous contact, communion or union with the Father within. This is the test of our prayer: if we make our inner contact, if we gain our "click," if we feel the gentle warmth within, we know that we have been experiencing effective prayer. Whenever this inner contact is not made, our prayer is in the realm of the letter of Truth, rather than in the realm of the Spirit of Truth, and it does not bear fruit of a spiritual nature. Again I quote from *The 1954 Infinite Way Letters*: "When we hear the still, small Voice of God, when we receive the inner impartation or the feeling of the Presence of God, we are receiving the benefit of prayer, and whatever may be the necessary *form* of demonstration will take place in our experience."

(A Student.)

The Ninth Commandment

The Ninth Commandment, "Thou shalt not bear false witness against thy neighbor," is a Cosmic Law, but what does it mean? Certainly this does not mean that we are just not to spread rumors and gossip about our neighbor, but that we are not to hold our neighbor in humanhood. If you say, "I have a fine neighbor," you are bearing false witness against him just as much as if you said, "I have a very bad neighbor," because you are acknowledging a state of humanhood, sometimes good and sometimes bad, but never spiritual.

To bear false witness against your neighbor is to declare that he is human, that he is finite, that he has failings, that he is something less than the very

Son of God, and so we violate Cosmic Law every time we acknowledge humanhood. Every time we acknowledge our neighbor as capable of being sinful, poor, sick or dead; every time we acknowledge him to be other than the Son of God we are bearing false witness against him.

In the violation of that Cosmic Law we bring about our own punishment. God does not punish us—we punish ourselves, because if I say, "You are poor," I virtually say, "I am poor." There is only one I and one Selfhood, and whatever truth I know about *you* is the truth about *me*. If I accept the belief of poverty in the world, that reflects itself upon me. If I say, "You are sick," or "You are unkind," I am accepting that there is a quality apart from God, a being apart from God, an activity apart from God, and in that way I am condemning myself, because there is but one Self, and ultimately I am punished by my own conviction—bearing false witness against my neighbor.

We come to a place of *not* bearing false witness against our neighbor when we come to the realization that the Christ is our neighbor; that our neighbor is a spiritual being, the Son of God, just as we are. He may not know it, and you may not entirely know it, but the truth is, I am Spirit, I am Soul, I am Consciousness. I am the very manifestation, the very expression of God, and so are you and so is your neighbor, whether he is good or bad, friend or enemy, next door or across the seas.

Cosmic Law is revealed throughout scripture, and in the Sermon on the Mount (Matt. 5, 6, 7) the Master gave us a guide and code of human conduct to follow while training and developing ourselves to Spiritual or Cosmic Consciousness. The Infinite Way does not deal with good humanhood, in and of itself, nor is it a correction of one's human conduct. It deals entirely with understanding the spiritual values of reality; in the adoption of a spiritual code which automatically results in good humanhood. Good humanhood is just a natural consequence of spiritual identification. It would be impossible to understand that Christ is the Soul, the Life of individual being, and then quarrel with your neighbor or slander him. We place all of our faith, trust and confidence in the Infinite Invisible, and we are not considering human circumstances or conditions. Then, when we do come to human circumstances and conditions, we see them in their true relationship. When we say, "Thou shalt love thy neighbor as thyself," we are not speaking of human love or affection or friendliness: we are holding our neighbor in spiritual identity, and later we come to see how that is carried out in the human picture.

ACROSS THE DESK
Aloha Oe:[1] *Its Meaning*

It's more than just an easy word for casual goodbye;
It's gayer than a greeting and it's sadder than a sigh;
It has the hurting poignancy, the pathos of a sob;
It's sweeter than a youthful heart's exquisite joyous
    throb;

It's all the tender messages that words can not
    convey;

[1] Reprinted by permission of the Author.

It's tears unshed, a longing for a loved one gone
away;
It's welcome to Hawaii and it's lingering farewell;
It's all the dear and silent things that lover's lips
can tell;
It's woven into flower leis and old Hawaiian songs;
It's frailer than a spider-web and strong as leather
thongs;

It's fresh as dew on ginger blossoms and older than
the moon;
It's in the little lullabys that native mothers croon;
It's said a hundred different ways, in sadness and in
joy;
Aloha means "I love you." So, I say "Aloha oe."
(From: *Hawaii Says Aloha*, by Don Blanding.)

Recent years have introduced Hawaii to all the
world, and Aloha is fast becoming a universal language. We now have the Aloha greeting and the
Aloha parties of farewell; the Aloha spirit and the
Aloha giving. And who in all the world can convey
the meaning of Aloha as Don Blanding? In his latest
book, *Hawaii Says Aloha*, Mr. Blanding makes us
feel this Aloha so truly that some of that spirit must
rub off on us.

When the world accepts the Spirit of Aloha it
will quickly open the inner door of consciousness to
the final revelation: The Spirit of Christ. Then there
will be no more world to save, no sick to heal, no
sinner to punish or reform. "Where the Spirit of the
Lord is, there is liberty."

As we are consciously filled through reading and

hearing the Word, we begin to let this Spirit of the Christ flow from us, as the citizens of Hawaii let the Aloha spirit flow from them, and then we attract the world which is seeking freedom from the burdens of "this world."

Remembering this passage of scripture, "Where the Spirit of the Lord is, there is liberty," we will give up the external seeking for demonstrations, the anxious concern for persons, things, conditions, and we will seek, Oh! so diligently, sacredly and secretly, for "the Spirit of the Lord," knowing that in finding It we will have found our freedom in God.

CHAPTER TEN

THE INVISIBLE NATURE OF YOUR LIFE

"Ye have sown much, and bring in little: ye eat, but ye have not enough; ye drink, but ye are not filled with drink; ye clothe you, but there is none warm; and he that earneth wages earneth wages to put it into a bag with holes. Thus saith the Lord of hosts; Consider your ways. Go up to the mountain, and bring wood, and build the house; and I will take pleasure in it, and I will be glorified, saith the Lord. Ye looked for much, and, lo, it came to little; and when ye brought it home, I did blow upon it. Why? saith the Lord of hosts. Because of mine house that is waste, and ye run every man unto his own house. Therefore the heaven over you is stayed from dew, and the earth is stayed from her fruit. And I called for a drought upon the land, and upon the mountains, and upon the corn, and upon the new wine, and upon the oil, and upon that which the ground bringeth forth, and upon men, and upon cattle, and upon all the labor of the hands."

(Hag. 1:6-11.)

GOD, the Infinite Invisible (your individual consciousness) is the Source and Fount of your being, from which flows the Water of Eternal Life. Therefore, your individual consciousness is the storehouse of infinite spiritual unfoldment, and out of the *enriched spiritual awareness* comes all the joys and blessings of a complete and satisfying life. When this consciousness is what we term human, it is barren: it lacks the substance and the elements from which spiritual or perfect harmonious demonstration must flow. Instead of coming into the realization that God is your consciousness, "ye run every man unto his own house"—unto your own sense of spirituality and wisdom and supply, and, in thus looking to your personal selfhood, find that regardless of what you draw from it, you receive no sense of permanent good or satisfaction. "Ye looked for much, and it came to little." We have all sown much, but have brought in little; we have worked hard, but have accomplished nothing; we have earned much, but have nothing to show for it. We eat, and hunger again; we drink, and thirst again; we acquire and experience all the material and pleasurable things of human life, but find no fulfillment or contentment. This is true of each individual in his humanhood. "Thus saith the Lord of hosts; Consider your ways. Go up to the mountain, and bring wood, and build the house; and I will take pleasure in it, and I will be glorified."

In the second Chapter of Haggai, verses 4-9, we read: "Yet now be strong, O Zerubbabel, saith the Lord; and be strong, O Joshua . . . and be strong, all ye people of the land, saith the Lord, and work: for I am with you, saith the Lord of hosts: According to the word that I covenanted with you when ye came out of Egypt, so my Spirit remaineth among you: fear ye not. For thus saith the Lord of hosts; Yet once, it is a little while, and I will shake the heavens, and the earth, and the sea, and the dry land; And I will shake all nations, and the desire of all nations shall come: and I will fill this house with glory, saith the Lord of hosts. The silver is mine, and the gold is mine, saith the Lord of hosts. The glory of this latter house shall be greater than of the former, saith the Lord of hosts; and in this place will I give peace."

In these passages we are instructed to go up into high consciousness, and work, and build a Temple of God—a consciousness of spiritual Truth. Every time we read and hear and meditate upon the Word of God we are filling ourselves with the substance from which this House of Spiritual Consciousness is built. Every time we turn to the Infinite Source and draw ourselves into that which brought forth all the glories of the earth we are fulfilling these passages, so that when we are faced with our sense of physical supply, be it silver or gold, health or happiness, we find that it is in God and not in ourselves, and therefore it is infinite. We also find that the more that flows out, the more there is left over; but when we think of it as being *ours* there comes a sense of finiteness and limitation, and regardless of how much we take in, there is never anything left over.

Once you come into the realization that God is individual consciousness, you will see that God does not send supply, *God is the supply*, and then you will understand that no one can lessen or deplete his supply. It was this realization of the infinity of supply that enabled the Master to feed the five thousand with only five loaves and two fishes, and have twelve basketsfull remaining. God is the supply, and when you have God you have the infinity of supply. When you have the forms of supply without the supply itself you have nothing, and even if you had a billion dollars but did not have God, you would have nothing. Often an individual with a consciousness of supply accumulates great wealth and lovingly leaves it to his children, who, not having a consciousness of supply, promptly run through it or lose it, and within a short time find themselves with nothing. That is the meaning of the saying, "From shirt-sleeves to shirt-sleeves in three generations." God has given each one a great opportunity to live by his own consciousness. Every man is supplied in accordance with his own state of consciousness, and every man will lack in accordance with his own state of consciousness. Sooner or later, people will learn the folly of accumulating money for their children, and will understand that they bless their children only in proportion as they help to develop their consciousness of supply.

As you begin to perceive that *God* is your individual consciousness, and that *God is infinite,* you begin to discern the nature of supply as that which is invisible, and no longer do you judge the amount of your supply by appearances. The fruit on the trees and the dollars in the purse are not supply: these are only the forms which supply assumes in your experience for your use. Wherever *I am,* supply is, and never has an individual who has known that supply is invisible, spiritual, omnipresent, been without supply, except in those occasional moments now and then when there may seem to be a temporary absence of the forms of supply. "Yet have I not seen the righteous forsaken, nor his seed begging bread."

In my youth I suffered more or less from ill-health, and consequently I was a bit more concerned about the subject of death than most people. However, I developed an avid curiosity and interest in life, and dreaded the day when I would have to leave it. One day, after I had been to the barber-shop, the distasteful thought of death came to me, when suddenly I received my first glimpse of immortality. It occurred to me that the hair and the finger-nails that had just been trimmed were already in the furnace, but it was of no concern to me because *I* was still there and all was well. That made a difference in my attitude, because I was able to see that it could just as well have been my hand or arm, but *I* would still be here. From then on it was not difficult to see that regardless of what happens to the body, *I* am still here, separate and apart from that experience, and my life, my consciousness, will continue to go forward. Just as you are separate and apart from your automobile, even while your automobile is carrying you across the mountains, so are you separate and apart from your body. At no point are you a part of the automobile: the automobile is just an instrument or vehicle for your use, but you have no personal identification with it. You are not a part of it; you and the automobile are always separate and apart from each other. God is immortal, God is eternal, God is your true identity, and as you follow this through you will learn that regardless of where your body is, "I", which *I am*, is permanently and eternally here. The nature of God, Consciousness, is a continued state of immortality, of eternal being, and that is what *I am*.

"*I*", individually, *am* a state of Divine Consciousness.

As I pursued this thought, further questions arose: Who am I? What am I? Am I that which is visible, or am I the invisible, which acts to produce visibly? It is not a matter of I *have* a life force, but of realizing I *am* that life force. I *am* the spiritual life force which is functioning from the within to the without, and that life force constitutes my true and individual being. This is equally true of the things that we call supply, such as money, food, clothing, housing. *You* are the invisible life force. Your body is one of the forms which you assume. Your dollars, your home, your business, are other forms which you assume, but *you* are the animating life force of your being, of your body, your home and your business. Just as you are the directive force of your automobile, so are you the animating force of your entire career. The more you realize this, the more it flows in infinite forms and varieties. It is all a matter of right identification, and on that hinges the entire secret of your harmonious existence.

That I *am*, which is immortal, is likewise infinite, and with this understanding you will realize that you are never exhausting your supply, your life, your strength, nor your span of years. The only "I" exists as God-consciousness, and to see God as the "I" of your being (your individual consciousness) ends the periods of drought in which not only your supply seems to vanish, but your body also. As you perceive this point of your true identity as the Consciousness which permeates the body, which uses the body as an instrument or vehicle, you will come into the experience that is witnessed every day in nature: the bark falls from the tree, new bark appears, but the tree remains. Through this activity of Truth in consciousness you will eventually see that daily this body dies, and daily it is renewed, and that always this body will remain in strength, in health, in vitality, and in youthfulness.

When you perceive that you exist as consciousness, from that consciousness is received the word that was covenanted when you came out of the Egypt of spiritual darkness and ignorance. This covenant is the word "I". "I will never leave thee, nor forsake thee." "Lo, I am with you alway, even unto the end of the world." As you emerge from darkness and ignorance into spiritual wisdom, one of the first experiences is an inner assurance of a Divine Presence. Practically everyone who has had a spiritual experience has received some form of a promise—an assurance of a Presence and Power, an assurance of life immortal, an assurance of supply and protection.

"My Spirit remaineth among you," is the first covenant that is made with us as we come out of our religious superstition and ignorance. The Spirit, Presence, Power and Consciousness of God remains with you, and you find that "the glory of this latter house shall be greater than of the former." Once the realization comes that "I" exist not as body, but as Principle, as Spirit, as the very Consciousness of God, then, out of that consciousness, this "house" is filled with glory. All that beforehand was covered with a drought is renewed, and "the years that the locust hath eaten" are restored. In this new consciousness, which is the realization of true identity, the Spirit of God, the Christ, is upon you.

As you attain the realization of your true identity as an invisible life, no longer do you identify what you see in the mirror with yourself. That is not "I"—that is body, and as you realize this your body begins to change and improve in form. Ignorantly we have been identifying this body as ourselves, and through this false identification have made this body look as it does; whereas, with right identification we quickly begin to change its nature so that ten years from now it will probably look younger than it does at the present time. In every case of realization this is true to some degree. Out of the consciousness of God cannot come age, limitation, weakness or death, and I have witnessed many people in the advanced years of eighty and ninety who were far, far from such appearance because of the degree of their realization of this Truth. It is merely a question of realizing oneself to be God-consciousness, rather than limited, human, material, mortal, finite consciousness.

Every real and permanent blessing that comes into your experience must come through a transformation of *your* consciousness—through an activity of Truth in *your* consciousness. After you have been taught, and lifted to some measure of realization, no longer must you be deceived by appearances, but be able to see through every human being, animal or growing thing, and know that what you are seeing is only the form or body—that the true Self is invisible to sight. There is an invisible activity of Truth in consciousness within each of us, and that activity of Truth is constantly renewing and providing all that is necessary for our earthly experience. There is only one Consciousness, and every individual is this same God-consciousness; therefore, the degree of your demonstration lies in the degree of your conscious realization of this Truth. Great changes begin to come into your life, and the lives of others, as you are able to recognize the Christ, the invisible, spiritual man of God in all whom you meet.

Healings are brought about between practitioners and patients only by the practitioner's realization that God is an infinite, eternal and harmonious Life, and that *God constitutes individual being*. It is all a matter of right identification, and a steadfast realization of this Truth is all that is necessary. If we think of each other as human beings who must be healed, corrected or improved, we are just practicing a form of materia medica. Healings take place when we withdraw from all attempts to heal, correct or improve, and abode in the realization that *God* is individual being; that *God* is the only identity; that *God* is the Source; and that *God constitutes your true being*.

"Cast away from you all your transgressions, whereby ye have transgressed; and make you a new heart and a new spirit: for why will ye die, O house of Israel? For I have no pleasure in the death of him that dieth, saith the Lord God: wherefore turn yourselves, and live ye." We all have the same substance, the same life, the same inner activity; but the degree of your individual realization of this Truth determines the degree of your demonstration of it. Your Source is infinite, but the degree of your realization of the infinite nature of your Source determines the degree of your outer expression. "And be not conformed to this world: but be ye transformed by the renewing of your mind, that ye may prove what is that good, and acceptable, and perfect, will of God."

The Secret Place of Realization

It is not necessary to take thought for your life (that is, consciously direct it) for the same reason that the tree does not have to take thought for producing its fruit: its spiritual identity, being God, operates without the necessity of conscious or anxious thought. This, of course, does not in any way mean that we are to stop planning and conducting our affairs in a normal manner, nor does it destroy the human mind and activities. It simply means that instead of humanly setting about to direct your affairs each day, the first step is to retire into a period of inner meditation, and in this silence and peace receive the assurance and awareness that the Infinite Invisible Spirit of God is working in you, for you and through you—then It will give whatever right thought, direction and guidance is needed for your experience.

Recently I received an urgent call from a student, and I asked that he wait one hour before going ahead with what he had in mind at that instant—wait, wait one hour, wait until I had received the assurance of the Presence of God. Always wait, meditate, ponder, until you receive that assurance, and then go ahead. Once you have learned the practice of meditation up to the point of contact before venturing on any of your daily affairs, you will find that you will be led to take the right human footsteps.

As the contact is made, the ever-available Presence of God takes over and reduces the human footsteps, and directs the steps you are to take. While you take them, It performs the work that is given you to do; It goes before you to prepare the way and to make the crooked places straight, to do everything necessary for your protection, guidance, direction and support. Once you come to the place of trusting the action of the Infinite Invisible, never will you take a human step without Its inner assurance, and then you can be certain that you are on the right path. Even if you should take a wrong step or make a mistake, it will be corrected before any damage can be done.

At times, in our class and lecture work, the period of meditation lasts much longer than is usually the case. There is a reason for this: the meditation did not come to the point of release, to the point where It had taken over, and so there had to be a period of patience and waiting. Should I begin to speak before It comes, the only thing you would hear would be my stored-up memory of Truth, in which there is no power whatsoever. I could talk for hours, but unless a message comes forth out of the Consciousness of God, imbued with the Spirit, it has no substance, no activity, no life, no healing. It would not be the Word of God: it would just be that which I remembered, and that is not the Bread of Life. In the words of the Master, "My doctrine is not mine, but his that sent me," and if I wait until the answer comes from within, the message is spontaneous. Although you may have heard the words before, the Spirit is flowing, and it is now the Word of God, which is quick and sharp and powerful. It is this Word of God which produces harmony in the visible world.

Before venturing forth upon your daily affairs, your function is to be sure that the blight of human consciousness does not touch your crop, but that you are imbued with the covenant that was given in the beginning: "Be not afraid, neither be thou dismayed: for the Lord thy God is with thee whithersoever thou goest."

God is Individualized Consciousness

Through perception of the Truth of Being, you learn that all power is in your own consciousness, and in your consciousness of that which is appearing to you. Power is never separate from consciousness, nor is it ever something "out there" in person, place, circumstance or condition. God (Divine, Infinite Consciousness, which is individual consciousness) is all authority, all power, all harmony. It is through this understanding that you become possessed of your dominion. This is not personal dominion—it is the Dominion of God, acting as individual consciousness.

It is incorrect to condemn other people or to blame a circumstance or condition for any error in your life's experience. Furthermore, it is incorrect to believe that it is something over which you have no control. The real fault lies at the door of ignorance of the Truth. Everything that occurs in your experience is the direct result of your own consciousness, so now is the time to cease blaming someone or something for your troubles and problems. Troubles and problems are but adjustments, and there must be adjustments if there is to be spiritual progress. *Your experience is your own state of consciousness unfolding*, whether it is the experience of your health, home, companionship, business or supply.

All power is in God, and since God is your individual consciousness all power is available unto you. As you entertain this Truth in consciousness it naturally follows that your consciousness manifests itself as what appears to be an improved person, place, circumstance or condition. Once you have learned this Truth it is inexcusable to continue permitting domination by anyone or anything in the outer. No experience can come to you except as the unfolding of your own consciousness, and once you realize that *all is God, unfolding and disclosing itself*, the experiences you attract to yourself are on the level of this realization.

It is only through your own personal realization that you are able to help others, so ask yourself this question: Do I really know God as the consciousness of my individual being? Your work is finished when you attain your sense of oneness with God, so endeavor to make today your day of conscious realization, and henceforth your entire life will begin anew. Past experience has nothing to do with it, nor age, nor lack. All that is needful is the sincere desire to let today be your day of conscious oneness with God, and when you have attained that sense of oneness you become a law of peace and harmony unto yourself, and unto all who come within range of your consciousness.

For the benefit of those who desire to help others, it is necessary to learn to leave them alone. Do not attempt to convey some benefit to the individual, because no appeal to the human intellect can convince another of Truth. *Let Truth touch those who are ready for it.* Do not take them into your thoughts at all. When you turn to God, God automatically becomes the contact to any individual on earth who may at that moment be participating in your experience.

You are dealing with a principle—a principle that will heal and save and reform. Remember, however, that this principle can operate only if and when you leave the individual (patient) out of your thoughts, and keep your mind stayed solely on the fact that God is the cause, the law, and the effect unto all that is. The secret of harmonious living lies entirely in the realization of God as individual consciousness, and once you understand that, you can trust every one to the government of his own consciousness. Let the individual rest in that Truth—"loose him, and let him go."

Suppose you were faced with the claim of a discordant organ or function of the body. Turn away from the claim, turn to the Father within, and ask yourself: Is health, activity, power, in any organ or function of the body? Is not the body, in its entirety, an effect of consciousness? Is not consciousness that which governs and controls? Is not consciousness God? Since God is the consciousness of the individual, God is the substance of the body, the function of the organs. God has control over all that appears as body or bodily function, and therefore harmony is an everpresent law. The moment you have realized this Truth, dominion has been proved over the discordant organ or function.

If the question is one of supply, turn away from the *appearance* and take up the subject of supply. Realize God as the consciousness of the individual, and that consciousness as the supply. If the question is one of separation, turn away from the appearance and realize God as oneness. *All* being present in God, the belief in the separation is dissolved. Thus, in meditation, is consciousness opened in specific directions.

Accept this spiritual principle: God is the Life, Soul, Mind, Intelligence, Substance and form of individual being. Realize that when you say "God" you are speaking of the consciousness of individual you and me, and this consciousness (God) then becomes the law of health, wealth, harmony and happiness unto all. Once, this Truth has been accepted as a principle, you automatically revert to it whenever faced with any erroneous appearance or claim. The person seeking help is not your consideration: he is merely the one who will receive the benefit. Your only interest is: *what is the principle involved?* Retain your interest solely in this universal Truth, and as you embrace it as such all those who come in contact with you are healed. Then your gratitude is not for the healing—your joy is for *the principle shown forth.*

All dominion is in God, all jurisdiction is in God, and if you are silent enough, still enough, It will be manifest. You have dominion over "this world," not as a presumptuous human but through the Grace of God, and you manifest and express and bring it forth only in silent awareness. No matter how high your human thoughts may be, they are not God's thoughts. God's thoughts come only in Silence—in the realization of God as individual consciousness, unfolding and disclosing Itself.

Dominion by God's Grace

"In the beginning God created the heaven and the earth. . . . And God said, Let us make man in our image, after our likeness: and let them have dominion over the fish of the sea, and over the fowl of the air, and over the cattle, and over all the earth. So God created man in his own image, in the image of God created he him; male and female created he them. And God blessed them, and God said unto them, Be fruitful, and multiply, and replenish the earth, and subdue it: and have dominion over the fish of the sea, and over the fowl of the air, and over every living thing that moveth upon the earth."

Thus, in the first chapter of Genesis, we learn that God created man in His own image and likeness, and that God gave man dominion over everything in life. There is an "I" within you—an "I", created in the image and likeness of God, which is your individual, spiritual identity—your true Selfhood, and it is this spiritual identity which has dominion over everything in life.

In our Prodigal Son experience we have wandered from our Father's House, and have set up a separate identity which is called Joel, John, or Mary. Thousands of years of false teachings and their resultant erroneous concepts have brought us under the belief that we are subject to things in the external realm: that we are controlled by the body; and that we are victims rather than masters of this personal selfhood. Gradually, we have relinquished a little dominion here and a little there, until much of the time we live in fear of persons, things and conditions, and of late we have even come to fear the thoughts of other people. The world would have us believe that we are not Children of God; the world would have us believe that we do not have dominion over the earth, the skies, and the waters. If you examine your own thought, you will soon see how many things you fear in the external realm, and then you will realize that you *do* permit the world to have dominion over your thinking, over your bodies and your experiences.

The ability to rise above the discords of human experience begins with an understanding of what you are in life, and one of the first steps in spiritual living is to understand the word "I". Silently, within yourself, speak the word "I". "I, Joel—I, John —I, Mary"—realizing that that "I", which you have declared, is the Spirit of God in man, the immaculately conceived Son of God, the Christ. Again, silently speak the words: "God, the Father; God, the Son. God is the Father; God is the Son; and God is manifesting and expressing Himself as the spiritual identity of your individual being. There is no such thing as dividing God into bits. God appearing is the infinity of God. When you say "God is Love," the whole of the Godhead is included in that statement. When you say "God is Mind," or "God is Life," you are speaking of the Allness of God. God cannot be divided or separated from Himself. God is revealing, unfolding and disclosing Himself as you, and therefore every quality, every attribute, and every activity of God is embodied within you.

As you close your eyes and say "I", remember— ". . . the Son can do nothing of himself, but what he seeth the Father do: for what things soever he doeth, these also doeth the Son likewise." And again, "I can of mine own self do nothing," but by the Grace of God I have dominion over everything, every condition, every circumstance. "A thousand shall fall at thy side, and ten thousand at thy right hand; but it shall not come nigh thee." By the Power of God "I" have dominion.

"There is nothing from without a man, that entering into him can defile him: but the things which come out of him, those are they that defile the man." In other words, nothing on earth can have dominion over you, but the state of your consciousness determines the degree of the harmony or inharmony in your experience. If you permit yourself to be influenced by beliefs of weather, climate, infection, contagion, supply, you make yourself victim of these things. If you fear the thoughts of other people, you make yourself the victim of anybody's thoughts. Whereas, the moment you assert your God-given dominion, you become the law unto your universe.

The secret of harmony is the activity of Truth in *your* consciousness, and so it is the degree of activity of Truth, or the lack of it, that determines the good or evil in your experience.

In Quietness and in Confidence

Heretofore much of the work of spiritual teachers has been based upon reading, stating, declaring and affirming Truth. Now we rise to a higher level in consciousness, where we learn the true nature of silence, of stillness, of quietness; where we constantly and consciously "listen" for Truth to utter Itself within us. "Be still, and know that I am God," and this silence declares the Presence of God, inseparable from your very being. This stillness reveals that neither man nor circumstance can have power over you, since That which declares Itself to be "I" within you is all power. That which reveals Itself in quietness and in confidence is God, the restorer of harmony in your existence.

It is not the thoughts you think, but the thoughts which unfold in the Silence that constitute your guidance and inner wisdom. It is not the thoughts you declare, but the consciousness of Truth developed through your inner receptivity that brings God-government into your experience. Thought is not a power in the creative sense. No matter how much you think, you cannot make two times two equal four: you can only become aware that two times two *are* four. Thought is the avenue by which you become aware of the divine realities that already exist.

The Silence is the creative principle of all existence. The Silence is the healing activity in individual consciousness. The Silence is power. There is but *one being*, Christ, and the Christ of your being is the Christ of all. In the Silence the Christ utters Itself unto Christ in the depths of Its own Being. In the Silence you become receptive to the voice of the inner Self, and as Truth expresses Itself in your listening ear you become aware of the healing influence, with signs following. Your receptivity to the Kingdom of God, which is God-consciousness, God-awareness, God-knowing, constitutes the healing atmosphere.

There is a difference between taking thought and taking no thought. Take thought, not for the things of "this world" but for the things of God. Take thought for God and the activity of God. Take thought for the spiritual universe, and keep your "conversation in heaven" by pondering, meditating, thinking upon the things of God. As you go about your daily affairs, open your mind as well as your ears, and think: "Speak Lord; for thy servant heareth," and in this conscious turning within, listening to the Spirit, keeping the contact open, you are enabled to live God-governed lives. The activity of Truth in your consciousness is the Light which dispels the darkness of human sense. In quietness and in confidence, in receptiveness and in silence, Love reveals Its comforting Presence, and assures you that "underneath are the everlasting arms," upholding and supporting you, even in trial and tribulation.

"The Lord thy God in the midst of thee is mighty; he will save, he will rejoice over thee with joy; he will rest in his love, he will joy over thee with singing."

CHAPTER ELEVEN

SUGGESTIONS FOR HEALING WORK

DURING a trip around the world in 1954, I met with many men who are willing to agree that people with all types and forms of religious backgrounds and teachings, and every method of approach, can unite in the realization of two things: first, the realization of God as individual being; therefore, our conscious union with God, our oneness with the Source of all Good. Second: the prayers of the Church cannot heal. One such man is Brother Mandus, who, after a spiritual experience, found that he was a healer, and who heads the World Healing Crusade which operates in Protestant Churches of all denominations throughout England, Ireland, Scotland, Wales and Holland. Brother Mandus is convinced that once people know that there is a healing power in spiritual Truth they will no longer be satisfied merely listening to sermons, and that eventually it will become necessary for the ministers of the Churches to attain the healing consciousness which will enable them to "go, and do thou likewise." Fruitage of that already is seen in that many ministers are studying to attain this healing consciousness, and just recently the Church of England held a conference to which all the well-known healers were invited to participate in order that the Church might learn how healing is accomplished.

Before our meeting last year, Brother Mandus had read the *Infinite Way Writings* and wrote me stating how thoroughly in accord he was with that teaching, and how closely it paralleled his own unfoldment. I answered his letter and a correspondence and friendship developed between us. After meeting him I came away with the feeling that Brother Mandus is *a state of realized consciousness* —God-consciousness, Christ-consciousness; and that whatever healing he does is not through what he says or how he says it, but through the state of consciousness that he is. Although his Writings would seem strange to us, yet in between and behind it all you can see how the same consciousness is appearing on earth in that part of the country, doing the work in that way, while it is appearing on earth in this part of the country, doing it in this way. Although his work, in its presentation, is entirely different than ours, the ultimate motive is the same, and in order that you may see how universal this message is, I should like to share a portion of a recent letter.

"My dear Joel,—I was very thrilled and deeply moved by your recent letter with its vibrant message of love, power and authority. I am with you all the way in your clear-sighted realization of God as the only power, the only activity; and that therefore there is no need to battle with the negative beliefs, which are, in themselves, only a belief in a selfhood apart from God. In fact, all negative situations only have power when we ourselves recognize and deepen our awareness of them by concentrating in a battle to overcome them. Certainly I know in my ministry of healing that the spontaneous healings take place when we effectively know our oneness in God in a complete abandonment of effort to overcome anything. We rest in the Divine, and therefore there can only be the Divine, in full and free and perfect expression. In God there is no sickness, therefore sickness cannot exist, except when we insist upon separating ourselves from the Divine to believe in false appearances.

It is so wonderful how the new realization is beginning to reach out to the masses. With you I see most wonderful possibilities of spiritual revival in our time, and by this I do not mean the old-fashion revival, but a new, stirring, vital revival which brings us all into the absolute Spirit, where the Almighty Power of God can blaze forth in perfect expression. What a wonderful age this is—never in history has there been such opportunity to bring millions of people into a central realization of their Divinity. It is such a comfort and strength to feel united with you in this oneness of Spirit, therefore oneness with each other. In Spirit, therefore, "all that I have is thine," and infinite powers and potencies are released in you and in me, and in all whose lives touch ours. I rejoice with you, and give thanks that it is so.

Great events are in the making, and you truly say that this will be a wonderful year. Bless you for writing, and my spirit fuses with yours long before these words can reach you in print. At this

moment I am absolutely at one with you, and
you know that God uses me to bless you, and you
to bless me, for He it is who doeth all the work.
A thousand blessings, and love from us all.

Yours devotedly,

Brother Mandus."

Does this not show forth a beautiful spirit of
oneness, and is this not a breaking-down of "my"
teaching and "thy" teaching, of this Church's teaching and that Church's teaching, into the realization
of the Truth that there is but one Spirit, and that
that Spirit will raise up your mortal body, even as
It raised up Jésus Christ from the dead? That Spirit
is not Jew nor Gentile, Christian nor Mohammedan,
Oriental nor Occidental—that Spirit is God Itself
permeating human consciousness wherever human
consciousness is willing to open itself without pre-
judice, without bias, without limitation, and realize
that this is the Spirit of God in me, working through
me for your blessing; that this is the Spirit of God
in you, working through you for my blessing, since
we are one in Christ Jesus.

Probably never before in history have so many
people been in agreement that what we are showing forth to the world is not somebody's personal,
copy-righted teaching or religion, separate and apart
from the basic teachings of God, but rather, that we
are showing forth the very Spirit of God Itself. The
wisdom of all ages is once again coming to light in
human consciousness, and for the first time literally
millions are being told and taught of *their individual
divinity. God* is your being, your Mind, your Spirit.

God is the only law, the only activity. *God* it is that unites us, so that whatever blesses one blesses all. Whatever Spirit, Presence or Power of God is made manifest in my individual experience becomes your individual experience the moment we consciously unite in and as one. This is true of every one who can open consciousness to this realization. Let us all unite in the realization that I am in the Father and the Father is in me, and that therefore you are in me and I am in you, and we are all together in the Father, united in oneness. The light of this wisdom is entering human consciousness all over the globe, hastening the day when the Kingdom of Heaven is to come on earth.

One of the most vital points in the entire Message of The Infinite Way, and one which is repeated again and again in all of the Writings, is the nature of error. This is a point on which the Churches of the world must ultimately agree, because this is what prevents their prayers from being healing prayers. The prayers of the Church cannot heal because sickness and sin do not exist as conditions, and therefore praying to God is not the way to heal them. God cannot heal or remove that which has no existence. Negative conditions do not exist —they only operate in proportion to our acknowledgment of them, and our determination to battle them. It is only as we relax in the realization of our union in God, of God, as one with God; only as we rest in the realization that God is individual being and identity, and even the substance of the body— only then can we take the next step into the understanding that negative conditions have no existence, but that they exist only as universal beliefs which individually we are accepting. If you are accepting sickness and negative conditions there is work for you to do, and that is to reject such beliefs, not by battling disease or resisting sinful or negative conditions, but by consciously realizing that neither disease nor sin has entity, substance, law, or continuity.

Most people do not realize that they give reality to the very conditions from which they desire to be free. As much as they would like to be free of erroneous thoughts and conditions, they persist in demonstrating more of the negative than of the positive. As an example, I would like you to follow me in this illustration: Let us pretend that a few of us are gathered together for an informal talk when the telephone rings and you hear: "I have just received a message that Joel is very ill." What is your response? You see me, you hear me, and, judging by appearances, you know that it is a rumor, and you are not a bit disturbed. However, suppose I was not in the room when the call was received? No doubt you would have said, "Joel has helped us, now let us help him," and then everyone would have tried to help—but it would have been just as much of a rumor. Even if I were ill and you had any idea that you had power to bring about a healing, you would have been unable to help me unless you were able to say, "That is only a rumor." If you could accept, in spite of appearances, the Truth that it is only a rumor, I would have an instantaneous healing, because your stating that it was only a rumor would have been based on your spiritual recognition that I have no Life apart from God, no

Mind, no Soul, no Spirit, no being, no body apart from God; and therefore, anything other than that which is true of God would be rumor, appearance, false belief.

This is exactly the way in which we give power to the sins and diseases that afflict us. When the rumor comes in the form of a pain in the body, or from someone else, we accept it as a fact *about which we must do something*. This, in itself, is dishonoring God, because if there is something to be done that God already has not taken care of, there is not much *you* can do. Whatever discords we are suffering, and whatever discords we are not meeting for those who turn to us, are due to the fact that we are accepting rumors as facts, and then trying to do something about them. Every discord comes as an appearance, a suggestion or a temptation to accept a selfhood apart from God; to accept a condition apart from God.

The entire secret of healing lies in one word—"reaction." If, when a call comes for help, you react with a smile and say, "Rumor, temptation, appearance, nonsense," beautiful healings are accomplished. But the moment you answer with concern, as if actually there were *something* to be overcome, removed, resisted, refuted, in that degree have you accepted battle, and once having taken up the sword you will have to fight it through to the end. It is for this reason that we often struggle with physical, mental, moral or financial conditions for long periods, because we are not handling them as rumors to be disregarded, but as conditions that must be overcome. Even though you see it with your eyes and hear it with your ears, that does not mean it is a fact. It is a picture, an appearance, a rumor. Visible or audible, it is still a world belief appearing for your acceptance or rejection. Whenever you receive a call, whether from your own body or from patient or student, the immediacy of your reaction, and the resultant ability to dismiss it as a rumor, is the degree of healing that is realized.

Ask, Seek, Knock

"Ask, and it shall be given you; seek, and ye shall find; knock, and it shall be opened unto you."

Part One

These words of the Master have raised the question among students as to whether or not we are contradicting them when we say, Ask not, Seek not. There is no contradiction: instead, there is another question—What *did* the Master mean when He said, Ask, Search, Knock? As we come to understand more fully the message of Jesus Christ, we will know that to Ask, to Seek, to Knock, is all part of spiritual developments, but not in the sense of the world's acceptance.

There are no vacuums, no lacks, no limitations, *no negative conditions of any kind in a God world.* There is no other world, except the false world of illusion which we have accepted and which, consequently, we hate, fear, or love. Only harmony exists in the God world. If this were not true, God would not be Something to be worshipped, sought, welcomed. If there were a single sin or disease or death in all the world, God would be responsible. Therefore, there are *rumors* of discords, *rumors* of disease, *rumors* of sin, and we accept them as if they were fact, and demonstrate them.

As long as the Church teaches her people to pray for persons and things, they will be deluded and misled by this concept of God and prayer. If the Church would open her doors that we might utilize the silence, the purity and the integrity established there by her own righteous motives, then we could enter and pray the prayer of Asking, Seeking, Knocking—not that the discords of the world be overcome, but that the inner Light showing forth the *harmonies* of God's world be revealed.

We may *seek* the consciousness of Truth. We may *ask* for a realization of God as individual being. We may *desire*, even struggle, to attain that mind which was also in Christ Jesus; but we may not ask, or seek, or knock for a thing or a condition in the external realm, whether it be a person, a healing, an enrichment, employment, or a home. Our work is not that of trying to save or heal or redeem the world, but the revelation of God as individual being, which shows forth the non-reality of that which is appearing as negative conditions.

On this point we must unite, and I rejoice when I meet men and women who are willing to agree that the spontaneous healing work takes place not when we are battling sin and disease or trying to overcome it, but when we are uniting in the consciousness of our oneness in and with God. Let us, therefore, seek the Kingdom of God. Let us knock at the door of consciousness that this inner Light be revealed. Let us ask for spiritual wisdom, and then we will understand the prayer that reveals the

Kingdom of God as intact, here and now, and that reveals the illusory nature of that which is appearing to us as the errors of the world.

There is hardly a day in which we do not accept a rumor about ourselves and about others. Usually, the rumor is not how good So-and-so is, but how sick, how sinful, how poor or how dead. Either we think it is too bad and we would like to do something about it (which is, of course, accepting the rumor at face value) or probably we think he deserved it. In either case we have accepted the rumor, and by such acceptance of a suggestion of a selfhood apart from God *we have deferred the day of our own salvation.* Every negative person or condition comes as a rumor or a temptation to believe in the actuality of a negative person or condition, and each time you do not immediately disregard such a rumor, by that much you delay your own spiritual unfoldment. What happens to the other fellow really is not too important, because sooner or later he must wake up for himself.

Each day you must learn to reject the rumors of negative conditions of mind, body and purse that would foist themselves upon your consciousness. This consciousness of Truth cannot be built in the moment. It is the work of eternity, and so time is of no importance. You will come into this awareness bit by bit, step by step. As the Hindu has said, it is like peeling an onion by removing one skin at a time. Although you may not seem to be making much progress, eventually the day comes when you discern the fact that "I and my Father are one," and all is well with me and the universe.

In this consciousness there is no longer a hitting up against fear of the error and the resultant wondering what you can do about it, because the rumor is met instantly it touches your consciousness. Once you accept it and feel that you are not equal to it, you have lost your opportunity in that particular case, and it is well that you ask help of a practitioner. But eventually you must realize that this is not a question of a practitioner—this is a question of a rumor to be accepted as a fact or to be dismissed. Every day is lost and wasted until you learn that every discord and inharmony in your own life or that of others comes only as a rumor, a temptation, a claim of a selfhood apart from God; a belief in a presence or power apart from God. This realization is not going to come in its fullness in a flash, but you are on the way once you have undertaken this realization. Then each day becomes a day of Asking, Seeking, Knocking—not for the things of this world but for the realization that Thy Grace is maintaining this universe in its original integrity, purity, perfection, eternality and immortality.

"For every one that asketh receiveth; and he that seeketh findeth; and to him that knocketh it shall be opened."

Part Two

Moses, David, and others of the great characters of the Old Testament taught the doctrine of one God, but, of them all, the inspired prophet Isaiah was most emphatic, and throughout the Book of Isaiah you will find his exhortations and counsel: "Thus saith the Lord the King of Israel, and his redeemer the Lord of hosts; I am the first, and I am the last, and beside me there is no God. . . . Fear ye not, neither be afraid: have not I told thee from that time, and have declared it? ye are even my witnesses. Is there a God beside me? yea, there is no God; I know not any. . . . I am the Lord, and there is none else, there is no God beside me . . . look unto me, and be ye saved, all the ends of the earth: for I am God, and there is none else."

Practicing the Presence of God is two-fold. It is not merely realizing God as one—the one law governing this universe, the one substance, the one cause, the one effect, but going further to the second point which we call "the nature of error." The human mind does not like this term, "the nature of error." The human mind would prefer a Pollyanna religion that goes about declaring "God is Love," meantime permitting the snake of universal beliefs to strike. You, individually, must learn not simply to ignore error: you must be willing to look it squarely in the face and know it for what it is—nothing, a rumor, a temptation, a universal belief in a presence and power apart from God. The human mind must be willing to awaken to the realization that these appearances of error *do exist*, and that they do have presence and power in our experience until such time as we learn the nature of them as illusion.

Years ago, somebody said to me, "What about the hospitals and cemeteries?" and at that time I had no answer. Now I know the answer—there will always be hospitals and cemeteries as long as people are unwilling to look the situations right in the eye and know that every one of those appearances has existence only as a universal mental belief, a suggestion of a selfhood apart from God, of a law apart from God, of a condition apart from God. As long as people are willing to believe that God is some great Power that can heal disease or enrich them, there will be no end to these things called hospitals and cemeteries. It is one thing to believe that there is a God that overcomes error but leaves you in the error; it is quite another thing to know that there is a God that is an infinite Good, beside which there is none else.

You, individually, must be able to comprehend the nature of that which has been appearing for generations as sin, disease and death. You must be able to realize that you have been accepting these rumors because you have not known Christ as the identity of every individual on the face of the globe. Once you know that, you can reject every rumor and dismiss it. Most metaphysicians go about declaring, "It isn't true; it never happened." It *is* true, and it *did* happen, but what harm can come to the Christ? Crucify It, entomb It, and see if It does not walk the earth again! There is no use denying the crucifix, no use denying the tomb, but what difference does it make? Is it a power? Is it a presence?

Is there an activity apart from God? Is there a Mind apart from God? Is there a Life apart from God? Is there a law apart from God? There are no other Gods but one, and that one is the *I am* of your being and of my being, and when a rumor comes to you of a selfhood apart from God you must be alert enough to look right at the Christ of God and know that Christ is the only identity of individual being. Only that realization constitutes an individual who is set apart from mortal beliefs; only one who has, in some measure, realized that Christ is individual identity, that each individual is the Child of God, can say, "What power is there in such rumors or beliefs?"

Let us therefore ask and seek and knock for more spiritual light, more spiritual wisdom, more spiritual consciousness. Let us always remember that we can pray, ask, seek, knock, *as long as it is for something not of this world*, because "this world" cannot be demonstrated spiritually.

Excerpts from The Infinite Way

"Why are we so slow in gaining our freedom from illness, discord and other material conditions? It is entirely because of our inability to grasp the great revelation that there is no reality to error.

"So much attention has been given to faith in God to do something for us; or to faith in a healer or teacher, that we have over-looked the great truth—error is not real—there is no matter.

"We are learning from physical scientists as well as metaphysicians that what has been termed matter is a misinterpretation of Mind. Mind is

God and God is Spirit, therefore all that exists is spiritual substance regardless of the name or nature ascribed to it by finite sense.

"God is the Mind of the individual, therefore all that can come to us as person, thing or condition is coming to us as Mind, in Mind and through Mind, and God, Mind, is the Soul of every individual; God, Principle, is the law of all action; God, Spirit, is the substance of all of which we are conscious.

"Through false education, which constitutes finite sense, we have come to fear certain individuals, things and conditions, not realizing that as these are coming to us through the avenue of consciousness they are all God-being, Mind-appearing, Spirit-substance. Material consciousness is the false finite sense which beholds the universe and man as limited; as being both good and evil. Spiritual consciousness is the awareness of the individual as God-being; as having only the Mind which is God and the body of Spirit. It recognizes the entire universe as Mind-appearing and governed by divine Principle. Spiritual consciousness is the ability to see beyond the appearance to Reality. It is the recognition and realization that as God is our Mind, all that appears to us is in and of God which is our only consciousness.

"Spiritual consciousness does not overcome or destroy matter or material conditions but knows that no such conditions exist which finite sense presents. It translates the appearance for us, revealing the true nature of that which is appearing.

"Spiritual consciousness lifts us above every human form of limitation and permits us to enter a larger sense of life, health and freedom. Where there is spiritual consciousness there is no bondage to person, place or thing and there are no limitations to our accomplishments."

(*The Infinite Way*, Joel S. Goldsmith, pp. 89-92.)

Realization of God

As much as I would like to bring you release from the thoughts and things of the world, this cannot occur until you have consciously known the letter of Truth, and then gone within your own consciousness for the actual experience of Truth. The only reason for reading books, hearing lectures and attending classes *is to lead up to the point of realization.* Nothing you have read, heard or studied is of any importance or benefit except in the degree of realization that is attained in meditation.

Knowing the Truth, reading and studying the Truth is but one part, and the least part, of the whole demonstration. Such endeavor exists entirely in the realm of thoughts or statements until God places His Seal upon it by giving you a moment of realization wherein you experience a feeling of assurance and release. Then and only then has the reading and studying been beneficial. You may declare all you have learned, you may remember or memorize every word, but you have accomplished nothing for yourself or for the world until, in meditation, the Presence of God has announced Itself by a feeling of assurance that tells you "It is done— All is well—I am with you." Regardless of all the Truth-knowing that takes place in your consciousness throughout the day and night, never be satisfied until you have gone into meditation and there experienced the inner peace that assures you that God is on the field.

The day is approaching when there will be a band of spiritual wisdom and spiritual consciousness encircling the globe, at which each individual will be able to Ask, Seek and Knock. Whatever degree of realized consciousness on the part of teacher or student anywhere in the world will go to form the fabric of this band, and then each one who Asks, Seeks and Knocks for spiritual light will find that he is attuned. Anyone who reaches out will touch my realized consciousness, your realized consciousness, which forms this united band. Then the world will not be saved one by one, but by thousands, and the realization will be swift and complete. But first there must be such as you and I, who, in our particular localized places, achieve this consciousness and release it to the world so that those touching that degree of realized consciousness can attain some measure of it (at least enough for their healing) and then go on to *practicing the presence of God.*

The degree of realization you attain in meditation is one of the fibres that comprise this band of spiritual consciousness, and so it is well at this time to overcome the sense of time and space. When, through meditation, you have achieved a sense of release from the thoughts and things of the world, what a wonderful atmosphere surrounds you! This consciousness of Truth is not confined to the moment, nor in the place where you find yourself. This consciousness is never confined to time or space, therefore you can return to this degree of realized consciousness at will.

In the light of this, may I suggest that you lay this book aside for a few moments, and that you now go within for a period of meditation that this lesson may become vital, alive and active in your consciousness.

Thanksgiving

As we approach the time for celebrating Thanksgiving Day, a natural question arises: As a student of The Infinite Way, for what shall I give thanks, and in what manner shall my thanksgiving be expressed?

What have you asked? What have you sought? At what door have you knocked? The Master admonishes us: ". . . seek ye first the kingdom of God, and his righteousness," and by that He meant that you were to seek the things of God; that you were to knock at the door of consciousness for the revelation of the Infinite, Divine Presence within you. Is this not what you have asked of God? Is this not what you have sought? Therefore, let your thanks be that you have achieved some measure of the realization of God. Let your thanks be that *the door of spiritual consciousness has opened and revealed God as the very nature of your own being*. Let your thanks be that the kingdom of God, which you have long sought, has been found—within yourself. Let your thanks be that that to which you have devoted your life has become an accomplished, realized state of being, here and now.

CHAPTER TWELVE

CHRISTMAS 1955

A CHRISTMAS message should be a message of peace. Our thoughts turn from the peace the world is seeking to the true peace—"My peace" which, when men are ready to receive it, comes with healing of mind and body. The world seeks a peace that can never be found while its sense of peace is but an absence or cessation of war. This peace, even when accomplished, is temporary, because it is based solely upon conferences and relationships between men and nations. True peace is achieved only as we lay down the armor of flesh; as we put up the sword of defense from the fears and hatreds of the world: as we cease warring with the conditions of earth. Lasting peace reigns only when men's relationship to man is based upon his relationship to God. Peace is realized as we find union with our fellowmen through the experience of God. Peace is attained as we behold the Son of God ruling first our lives and then our neighbor's. The world is seeking peace "out there" but peace is to be found in entertaining the Prince of Peace within our own individual beings. Let us, therefore, no longer seek the peace the world is seeking but, rather, "The peace of God which passeth all understanding." "Peace I leave with you, my peace I give unto you: not as the world giveth, give I unto you. Let not your heart be troubled, neither let it be afraid."

"Behold my servant, whom I uphold; mine elect, in whom my soul delighteth; I have put my spirit upon him: he shall bring forth judgment to the Gentiles. He shall not cry, nor lift up, nor cause his voice to be heard in the street. A bruised reed shall he not break, and the smoking flax shall he not quench: he shall bring forth judgment unto truth. He shall not fail nor be discouraged, till he have set judgment in the earth: and the isles shall wait for his law. Thus saith God the Lord, he that created the heavens, and stretched them out; he that spread forth the earth, and that which cometh out of it; he that giveth breath unto the people upon it, and spirit to them that walk therein: I the Lord have called thee in righteousness, and will hold thine hand, and will keep thee, and give thee for a covenant to the people, for a light of the Gentiles; To open the blind eyes, to bring out the prisoners from the prison, and them that sit in darkness out of the prison house. I am the Lord: that is my name: and my glory will I not give to another, neither my praise to graven images. Behold the former things are come to pass, and new things do I declare: before they spring forth I tell you of them."

(Isa. 42:1-9.)

"The Spirit of the Lord God is upon me; because the Lord hath anointed me to preach good tidings unto the meek; he hath sent me to bind up the brokenhearted, to proclaim liberty to the captives, and the opening of the prison to them that are bound; To proclaim the acceptable year of the Lord, and the day of vengeance of our God; to comfort all that mourn; To appoint unto them that mourn in Zion, to give unto them beauty for ashes, the oil of joy for mourning, the garments of praise for the spirit of heaviness; that they might be called trees of righteousness, the planting of the Lord, that he might be glorified. And they shall build up the old wastes, they shall raise up the former desolations, and they shall repair the waste cities, the desolations of many generations. And strangers shall stand and feed your flocks, and the sons of the alien shall be your plowmen and your vinedressers. But ye shall be named the Priests of the Lord: men shall call you the Ministers of our God: ye shall eat the riches of the Gentiles, and in their glory shall ye boast yourselves. For your shame ye shall have double; and for confusion they shall rejoice in their portion: therefore in their land they shall possess the double: everlasting joy shall be unto them. For I the Lord love judgment, I hate robbery for burnt offering; and I will direct their work in truth, and I will make an everlasting covenant with them. And their seed shall be known among the Gentiles, and their offspring among the people: all that see them shall acknowledge them, that they are the seed which the Lord hath blessed. I will greatly rejoice in the Lord, my soul shall be joyful in my God; for he hath clothed me with the garments of salvation, he hath covered me with the robe of righteousness, as a bridegroom decketh himself with ornaments, and as a bride adorneth herself with her jewels. For as the earth bringeth forth her bud, and as the garden causeth the things that are sown in it to spring forth; so the Lord God will cause righteousness and praise to spring forth before all the nations."

(Isa. 61.)

"For Zion's sake will I not hold my peace, and for Jerusalem's sake I will not rest, until the righteousness thereof go forth as brightness, and the salvation thereof as a lamp that burneth. And the Gentiles shall see thy righteousness, and all kings thy glory: and thou shalt be called by a new name, which the mouth of the Lord shall name. Thou shalt also be a crown of glory in the hand of the Lord, and a royal diadem in the hand of thy God. Thou shalt no more be termed Forsaken; neither shall thy land any more be termed Desolate: but thou shall be called Heph-zibah, and thy land Beulah: for the Lord de-lighteth in thee, and thy land shall be married."

(Isa. 62:1-4.)

"And they shall call them, The Holy people, The redeemed of the Lord: and thou shall be called, Sought out, a city not forsaken."

(Isa. 62:12.)

Oftentimes the admonitions and promises of the Old Testament prophets are misinterpreted as per-taining to some particular man or to a specific race or nation. The ancient Hebrews called themselves the Children of God, and considered themselves a race set apart and favored by God. Such misapprehensions have led to the worship of certain so-called saviors as if they themselves were the Christ, and this, in turn, to denominational religions with their limiting differences and enmities. God has not anointed a certain man or a special people: God has anointed His Beloved Son, the Christ. The Christ is a spiritual entity, a spiritual impulse—a Spirit that is in man, and He it is that is blessed, anointed, upheld by the Father.

Occasionally this Divine Spiritual Impulse, the Christ, appears as more pronounced in an individual here and there, but It exists in the consciousness of every individual on the face of the globe. There comes a specific period in the life of each individual when he comes to the place of spiritual annunciation in which the Christ is conceived, nurtured, developed, until, on Christmas Day, the Child is born; or, in other words, the Presence of the Christ is realized. The birth of the Christ does not chronologically occur on the twenty-fifth of December, nor geographically in the Holy Lands, but, rather, it takes place in the uplifted consciousness of the individual. It is this uplifted consciousness that is the Holy City—the city that is called "Sought out". —the birthplace and dwelling place of the Christ. Wherever this Spirit of God appears in human consciousness, all the blessings and prophecies regarding the rich fruitage of the Christ are made evident.

In the light of the Christ the human scene is revealed as somewhat fantastic. It is only after the Christ has been realized in consciousness that the depth of true humility is understood. Before that time there is always a sense of personal ego, but with the birth of the Christ all sense of personal demonstration or the desire for any person or thing, accomplishment or achievement is lost. One comes to a point of transition in consciousness from that place where there exists a need, a desire, or an unfulfilled life, to that place where there is no life of one's own to be fulfilled, made happy, prosperous or content. There no longer exists even a sense of needing God because there is a realization of *God acting through one.* This activity is never for one's personal benefit, but is a blessing unto those who have not yet experienced the conception and birth of the Christ within their own being and thereby realized the universal nature of the Christ.

Elijah revealed the nature of the Christ as a still, small Voice which is within the realm and reach of every individual who attains the receptive ear. Daniel revealed the Christ as a stone "cut out of the mountain without hands." In the words of Isaiah: "He shall not cry, nor lift up, nor cause his voice to be heard in the street. A bruised reed shall he not break, and the smoking flax shall he not quench: he shall bring forth judgment unto truth." When the Master spoke of those who have eyes but do not see and those who have ears and do not hear, He was speaking of an inner capacity that beholds that which the human eye can never behold, hears that which the human ear can never hear, knows that which the human mind can never apprehend. The nature of the Christ is a spiritual activity, wholly without physical accomplishment, yet It is sufficient to destroy the four temporal kingdoms.

Within me there seems to be a swiftly moving mountain stream which, from many directions, is being joined by smaller streams. United these flow as one stream in a turbulent yet orderly progress toward the sea. The words and thoughts of Elijah, Daniel, Isaiah, Jesus and others of the great Biblical characters are rushing into my inner being, and there uniting in the revelation of one spiritual Essence, one Presence, one Power. Intermingled with this are thoughts of the many children who have come into this life crippled or otherwise handicapped. These children, with their cry "Why? Why this? Why me?" are surging in on the earth consciousness, but the earth has no answer to their problem, no answer to their healing. Likewise, a similar cry is going up from people the world over for a cessation of war and a world peace, and the earth has no answer to them. *But there is an answer!* The answer is Christ!—Christ, a spiritual influence within you, within me, and within all whose hearts and Souls are open to the annunciation, to the experience of conception and birth of the Christ. The Spirit of the Lord God Almighty is upon the Christ of your individual being, and this gentle Presence, achieved "not by might nor by power," is the anointing of the Spirit Itself. It is this Christ that is the answer to world peace, and It is an answer also to those little ones who are clamoring for their divine heritage of harmony and wholeness.

"He shall not fail nor be discouraged, till he have set judgment in the earth." The ultimate mission of the Christ is the healing of the world; therefore it becomes necessary for those who have felt the touch of the Christ to make way for Its activity to permeate human consciousness. Prayer is the avenue or activity of our consciousness which brings the Presence and Power of God into human affairs. Eventually, you will come to that place in consciousness where you will receive requests for specific help, and in order to be prepared it is necessary that you learn to entertain the Prince of Peace for no other purpose than the communion itself; each day you must have at least one period of meditation devoid of any problem concerning your own personal life, for the sole purpose of experiencing in consciousness a communion with God. In this communion the activity of the Christ within you is a specific healing to whoever has requested help.

Recently, I received a photograph of a beautiful young child, together with a letter from a minister stating that this child had been born deaf and dumb, and thus a specific request came to my desk for the healing of that child. It is not necessary to tell you that with all the hope, faith and confidence of my being I turn to the Christ, the anointed One within me which has received the Spirit of God upon It. I turn to this healing consciousness in order to let It be released into the world for the purpose of reaching that child. Is there any other hope for that child than that the Christ Itself be loosed in consciousness, be revealed, unfolded, disclosed, so that That which carries the Presence and Power of God into the world may have Its effect upon that young life?

Just think of the healing consciousness that can be brought to the world as each Infinite Way student realizes, first of all, that "the only begotten Son, which is in the bosom of the Father" is the Christ of his individual being! All that the Father hath is bestowed upon this vital, living, eternal, immortal Child, and Its abiding place is within you, in your consciousness! And always remember that "where two or three are gathered together in my name. there am I in the midst of them." The gentle activity of the Christ in the midst of you is sufficient to the tearing down of the four temporal kingdoms. But one thing is required—Christ must have Its Jesus! The spiritual Child must have Its representation on earth, and It must be released to the world through the consciousness of those individuals who have come to realize Christ in the midst of them.

Other than to be aware that such conditions exist, it is not necessary for you to know of specific cases of these handicapped children. Instead, it is your function, daily and without fail, to go within for the purpose of receiving the Prince of Peace, thereby permitting entrance of the Christ into human affairs. It is not necessary to direct or enlighten It in any way, but just to wait—silently, without effort, without power—*and let it occupy consciousness*! Can you not see what will happen when the Christ, really realized, begins to touch the consciousness of all the peoples of earth, removing from them the causes and effects of human error? The Christ touching your consciousness and freeing you from the hates and fears of the world will bless countless others. Prayer, from this standpoint, is an opening of yourself to the visitation and communion with the Prince of Peace, and makes of your consciousness the Holy City where dwells the Christ, and through which the Christ finds entrance into human consciousness.

Wherever in scripture there is a realization of the coming of the Christ there is also the prophecy of the crucifixion. These prophecies have nothing to do with any particular savior or redeemer, but with the birth of the Son of God in individual consciousness. There is in the human nature that which does not wish to be overthrown, and it knows there is but one power that can annihilate human nature and that is the Presence of the realized Christ. Always the world seeks to destroy the Christ, and it is for this reason that soon after the experience of realization there occurs a period known as "going down into Egypt and hiding the Babe," during which one refuses to reveal It lest the world, in its thoughtlessness, destroy one's confidence and assurance in Its Presence and Power. It is surprising with what subtlety and cunning the sense of anti-Christ can enter consciousness, sometimes undermining one's faith to the extent of making one doubt or deny ever witnessing or experiencing a healing.

It is for this reason that I continually caution students not to be too hasty or too revealing in their speech and actions, but to wait until the activity of the Christ becomes so firmly established, so beautifully developed as the very activity of consciousness that there is no longer any fear, no longer any doubt. Then you can stand before the world and reveal It, and even take whatever manner of scorn or doubt the world may offer and be not at all concerned nor affected by it. While we, ourselves, are presenting the Christ, we are in danger of losing It. When the Christ has sufficiently taken over, It presents Itself so silently, so secretly that no one of the world knows or recognizes what It is, and yet Its influence and effect can be felt by all.

As this message is being written, I sit back for a moment of meditation, and instantly there seems to be a Presence, much like an actual figure, within my consciousness, yet One not restricted or entombed in flesh. This Presence is abroad in the world, carrying Its own power of peace and healing; opening the eyes of the blind, releasing the prison bars, illuming man's consciousness so that he may no longer be in darkness, but that he may know the Divine Grace which accompanies the Son of God.

"Behold my servant, whom I uphold; mine elect, in whom my soul delighteth; I have put my spirit upon him: he shall bring forth judgment to the Gentiles." Behold this gentle Presence within you, receiving Its Grace from the Godhead Itself; dispelling the sense of I, me, mine; effacing the sense of personal possession and accomplishment in the realization that "The earth is the Lord's and the fulness thereof. . . . Son, thou art ever with me, and all that I have·is thine."

As long as the vine is receiving its sustenance from the Father, every branch is being fed. The Holy One of Israel, the Spirit of God in man, the Christ, is always present, but available only as we open ourselves to receive It, to abide with It. We do not entertain the Christ that we may be fed, clothed, housed, or otherwise benefited: we enter meditation for the sole purpose of communion with the Holy One of Israel, so that the Christ may find outlet through us, thus tearing down the mighty strongholds of human belief and establishing God's Kingdom on earth. There is no personal work to be done in this communion—*we have only to be still, and let it flow out!* In the true sense of humility there is no "I" directing this activity; instead, there is a feeling of deep peace and quiet, in which we are perfectly willing to let It be about the Father's business. Never are you and I about the Father's business—only the Christ performs the functions of God on earth, establishing His reign in the hearts of all who are receptive and responsive to Its healing Presence.

"The place where thou standest is holy ground" —Jerusalem, the Holy City, whenever you entertain the Prince of Peace; whenever the Christ fills your consciousness and thereby finds outlet to all the world. And so, on Christmas Day, we bid Godspeed to the Prince of Peace on Its Journey of Love into human consciousness, so that each individual whose thought and mind, Spirit and Soul are open to the conception and birth of the Christ may know this gentle Presence, which is capable of bringing peace on earth, good will towards men.

The Lamplighters

"I and my Father are one," but only in the degree that we are aware of this oneness can our spiritual

235

integrity be maintained. As long as it can be made to appear that there is a you here, separate and apart from God, and a God "out there" somewhere, separate and apart from you, just that long can inharmonies and discords beset your path. The infinitude of God includes all being! Nothing is more important to know and to understand. It is the secret of all ages, the foundation of all religions. No religion and no Truth would be worthy of the names did they not clearly reveal the fallaciousness of an infinite God *and something else*.

The sun and the sunbeam are one, the sun itself —the sunbeam is the sun's way of appearing to us. Just so, you and I, as individual beings, are one with God—God appearing as your form and as mine. You can no more escape from God, Good, than the sunbeam can escape from the sun. Just as warmth and light are constituent elements of the sunbeam, so are Life, Truth, Love, harmony, peace, joy and dominion constituent elements of your being. Eternality and immortality are constituent principles of your being, and you can no more be deserted by eternality and immortality than God can be bereft of Itself.

Every individual is that center of Consciousness through which, or as which, the infinite Good of God is pouring Itself into the world. All that God is, and all that God has, is pouring Itself through you to me, and in like manner all that is in and of God is pouring Itself through me to you. All that we call Truth, all that we call Life, all that we call Love, all that we call Spirit, is manifesting and expressing Itself as individual being. "Ye are the light of the world"—that God-light which is manifesting Itself to all mankind.

Just think of the infinity of Good which, at this very moment, is pouring Itself through you and through me, and then consider what that means in our relationship to the world. Does that not make us all one in Christ? Does that not make us all one in Truth? Does that not make us "heirs of God, and joint-heirs with Christ"? Does that not make us all fellow-citizens of the household of God. Does that not make us all friends? As we recognize our oneness with God, automatically we recognize our oneness with all others. But we must make the acknowledgment; we must call each other friend— even those who appear as enemies. Friend or enemy, each is the light unto the other. When we find our oneness with God we find our oneness with every bit of good belonging to our fellow-man, to our unfoldment, to our expression.

The function of the human teacher is just to be an avenue, a vehicle for God; to open your consciousness to the receptivity of Truth, so that thereafter you may receive Truth directly from within your own being. The teacher may have received the Light just a moment before sharing that Light with you, and you, in turn, immediately begin to share with your friend. "No man, when he hath lighted a candle, covereth it with a vessel, or putteth it under a bed; but setteth it on a candlestick, that they which enter in may see the light."

A Jesus, a John, a Paul may come into your experience to carry the message of Truth, but even without these you will not be left without guidance.

"I will not leave you comfortless: I will come to you." As you relax from the stresses of the world this "I" in the midst of you will reveal the full Truth of being. "But the Comforter, which is the Holy Ghost, whom the Father will send in my name, he shall teach you all things, and bring all things to your remembrance, whatsoever I have said unto you." In the end, all shall be taught of God.

"Ye are the light of the world. A city that is set on an hill cannot be hid," and as you realize this Truth you become a Light in your home and in your community. And the moment you recognize that Light in friend or neighbor—wherever there is a receptive thought—you kindle the Light in him. That makes you a lamplighter. That is what we all are—lamplighters—and so let us remember the gentle words of the Master: "Let your light so shine before men, that they may see your good works, and glorify your Father which is in heaven."

The True Source of All Good

"Now faith is the substance of things hoped for, the evidence of things not seen. . . . Through faith we understand that the worlds were framed by the word of God, so that things which are seen were not made of things which do appear. . . . But without faith it is impossible to please him: for he that cometh to God must believe that he is, and that he is a rewarder of them that diligently seek him."
(Heb. 11:1-3-6.)

By faith we mean that quality of spiritual consciousness which discerns even without physical

238

evidence. Through spiritual discernment we apprehend and comprehend those things which the human mind cannot understand. Through spiritual consciousness we know that that which appears as visible form was made by that which is, and always will be, invisible to human sense. By faith, or spiritual discernment, we know that the world of form is an emanation of the invisible substance called Life, or Spirit, or God.

By faith, or spiritual awareness, we know that the inner Invisible is infinite, and that therefore the world of creation is infinite, forever unfolding and disclosing itself in infinite form and variety, character and nature. Because of the infinite nature of the Invisible, we spiritually discern the infinite nature of creation, and never become dependent upon anything that has form, because, knowing its Source and realizing the infinite nature of the Source, we are enabled to understand the infinity of the creation of form. The Source or substance of all creation is this Infinite Invisible Soul or Spirit, and through this understanding we realize that there is nothing of a destructive or evil nature in creation.

The seeker after spiritual wisdom, while grateful for all forms of creation, and happy to make use of and enjoy all manifestations, soon finds it impossible to feel dependent upon person, thing or condition. Starting with happiness, ordinarily an individual's happiness is dependent upon some person, circumstance, condition or thing, and when there is an absence of that which would arouse the sense of happiness, unhappiness is the result. The first lesson that must be learned is that happiness must not be made dependent upon person or thing, nor must unhappiness be permitted to follow the absence of person or thing. The seeker must reach a state of consciousness in which happiness springs from an inner illumination, an inner awareness which, in scripture, is called faith—the spiritual discernment of the nature of all effect through understanding the nature of cause. The seeker must be given ample time in which to transfer his happiness from that which appears in the outer, to the spiritual discernment of the inner. Progress is being made when happiness is evident without regard to the world of appearances.

This same lesson also applies to supply. In most cases, supply is dependent upon labor, investment, marriage, inheritance, etc. Spiritually, supply is understood to be the outward appearing of the infinite inner Invisible. The student must be given opportunity for making the transition from dependence upon money, to the realization of supply as the emanation of that which is already established within.

Health usually is understood as being dependent upon the normal functioning of the organs and functions of the body, but now the transition must be made to an understanding that health is a quality and an activity of Soul, Spirit, Life, manifesting and expressing as the harmony of the body. This eliminates fear when inharmonious conditions of body and health are met.

Peace, which ordinarily means absence of war, is no longer a condition of human conduct, but, rather, peace is understood as a state of the Soul—

a continuing, permanent, eternal and immortal state of the Soul, never dependent upon outer conditions. Peace must first be sought within, then peace will appear without.

When the disciples were concerned about the Master, He said unto them: "I have meat to eat that ye know not of." And the same thought was conveyed by Paul: ". . . the kingdom of God is not meat and drink; but righteousness, and peace, and joy in the Holy Ghost." The understanding of this wisdom will free you from all dependence on person, place, thing, circumstance or condition; and yet, will add to you the infinity of God, appearing as all the good things of this world.

A Beholder

God pours Itself forth as Life, Love and Truth. It is your function to be a beholder—*to let God express Itself*, while you watch the activity and enjoy it.

Never personalize. As soon as you try to restrict or limit God to a specific person or channel, it is as if you would limit the sun to a specific garden. Look above your own garden—see the warmth and light of the sun, and delight in its universality, impartiality and impersonality.

So it is with Life—look above Its forms and see It, *omnipresent as all form*. So it is with Love— look away from person, and behold Love appearing through all. In this way you do not limit Love coming only through family and friends, but through any whom Grace may select. So it is with Truth— look above all teachings so that you do not limit Truth to certain teachings or religions, and thereby behold Truth through infinite avenues or instruments.

The New Dimension—Christ

There is a certain spiritual groove, or inner rhythm in consciousness, into which we (individually) fit; and when so located find ourselves in outer circumstances, places and conditions of eternal peace and harmony. This is not a static peace, but a vital state of spiritual being and activity.

At times this peace is a deep stillness within, resulting in quiet and joy in worldly affairs. Again it may appear as warfare, since ". . . I came not to send peace, but a sword." This warfare represents our painful surrender of self, and our ultimate realization of spiritual Selfhood and harmony. It is the laying off of the cocoon in order that the butterfly may emerge.

In meditation, in quiet contemplation of the Soul, we achieve or attain this groove or rhythm in consciousness and then, and only then, do we know the government and realm of Spirit. No longer are our values based on material estimates but, instead, are measured by the standard of "My kingdom"—Love. In this rhythm of consciousness we rest in the Soul, and find recompense and activity in the new dimension—Christ.

PUBLISHER'S NOTE

Joel Goldsmith wrote over forty books and essays over the many years of his teaching activities. All Goldsmith writings currently in print are available from DeVorss & Company.